CRITICAL ESSAYS ON

EMMA

Editors:
Linda Cookson
Bryan Loughrey

LONGMAN
LITERATURE
GUIDES

Longman Literature Guides

Editors: Linda Cookson and Bryan Loughrey

Titles in the series:

PREFACE

Like all professional groups, literary critics have developed their own specialised language. This is not necessarily a bad thing. Sometimes complex concepts can only be described in a terminology far removed from everyday speech. Academic jargon, however, creates an unnecessary barrier between the critic and the intelligent but less practised reader.

This danger is particularly acute where scholarly books and articles are re-packaged for a student audience. Critical anthologies, for example, often contain extracts from longer studies originally written for specialists. Deprived of their original context, these passages can puzzle and at times mislead. The essays in this volume, however, are all specially commissioned, self-contained works, written with the needs of students firmly in mind.

This is not to say that the contributors — all experienced critics and teachers — have in any way attempted to simplify the complexity of the issues with which they deal. On the contrary, they explore the central problems of the text from a variety of critical perspectives, reaching conclusions which are challenging and at times mutually contradictory.

They try, however, to present their arguments in a direct, accessible language and to work within the limitations of scope and length which students inevitably face. For this reason, essays are generally rather briefer than is the practice; they address quite specific topics; and, in line with examination requirements, they incorporate precise textual detail into the body of the discussion.

They offer, therefore, working examples of the kind of essay-writing skills which students themselves are expected to develop. Their diversity, however, should act as a reminder that in the field of literary studies there is no such thing as a 'model' answer. Good essays are the outcome of a creative engagement with literature, of sensitive, attentive reading and careful thought. We hope that those contained in this volume will encourage students to return to the most important starting point of all, the text itself, with renewed excitement and the determination to explore more fully their own critical responses.

How to use this volume

Obviously enough, you should start by reading the text in question. The one assumption that all the contributors make is that you are already familiar with this. It would be helpful, of course, to have read further — perhaps other works by the same author or by influential contemporaries. But we don't assume that you have yet had the opportunity to do this and any references to historical background or to other works of literature are explained.

You should, perhaps, have a few things to hand. It is always a good idea to keep a copy of the text nearby when reading critical studies. You will almost certainly want to consult it when checking the context of quotations or pausing to consider the validity of the critic's interpretation. You should also try to have access to a good dictionary, and ideally a copy of a dictionary of literary terms as well. The contributors have tried to avoid jargon and to express themselves clearly and directly. But inevitably there will be occasional words or phrases with which you are unfamiliar. Finally, we would encourage you to make notes, summarising not just the argument of each essay but also your own responses to what you have read. So keep a pencil and notebook at the ready.

Suitably equipped, the best thing to do is simply begin with whichever topic most interests you. We have deliberately organised each volume so that the essays may be read in any order. One consequence of this is that, for the sake of clarity and self-containment, there is occasionally a degree of overlap between essays. But at least you are not forced to follow one — fairly arbitrary — reading sequence.

Each essay is followed by brief 'Afterthoughts', designed to highlight points of critical interest. But remember, these are only there to remind you that it is *your* responsibility to question what you read. The essays printed here are not a series of 'model' answers to be slavishly imitated and in no way should they be regarded as anything other than a guide or stimulus for your own thinking. We hope for a critically involved response: 'That was interesting. But if *I* were tackling the topic . . .!'

Read the essays in this spirit and you'll pick up many of the skills of critical composition in the process. We have, however, tried to provide more explicit advice in 'A practical guide to essay writing'. You may find this helpful, but do not imagine it offers any magic formulas. The quality of your essays ultimately depends on the quality of your engagement with literary texts. We hope this volume spurs you on to read these with greater understanding and to explore your responses in greater depth.

Pat Pinsent

Pat Pinsent is Principal Lecturer in English at the Roehampton Institute of Higher Education.

ESSAY

'There is a whole larger world outside, of which she says nothing.' Discuss this view of Jane Austen in relation to *Emma*

What is this larger world which Jane Austen's *Emma*, published in 1816, is presumed to ignore? The very date draws to our attention the fact that she must have been writing it while the Napoleonic Wars came to the climax of Waterloo. This decisive event, like the unrest in England triggered by the French Revolution more than twenty years previously, is absent from our consciousness as we read. Instead we have the insularity of Highbury, which seems more remote from London, only sixteen miles away, than the Western Isles of Scotland would be today. All that matters is who is marrying whom, within the genial babble of Miss Bates's gossip. That Austen is a great moralist is universally acknowledged, but that her subject is a miniature one seems almost unquestioned. It is my intention, however, to show how effectively she does comment on the 'larger' world, and to demonstrate that *Emma* is firmly grounded in the social issues of its time, revealing that its writer is as perceptive about these as she is about the nuances of polite society. While the incidents on which I will draw are often inevitably those which others have also used to display Austen's skill in exploring character and small-scale moral action, I propose to show how they form part of a larger perspective.

In *Emma*, as to some extent in all her novels, Austen puts forward her view of the necessity for stability, for a responsible, *rooted*, ruling class, informed by compassion for those in need, and either governing their estates with due consideration (a duty with aspects applicable to the women as well as to the men) or following a profession with diligence. Those who have not inherited estates but have acquired them through their own hard work or through commerce should take on, with their property, the responsibilities it brings — Mr Weston (chapter 2) is one who shows this admirably. The owners of the greater properties, Hartfield and Donwell (chapter 16) have, however, more responsibility than he has, though Mr Woodhouse has abdicated his in favour of Emma, who dominates Highbury society because of her social standing rather than her intellectual superiority, marked though this is. Her power is everywhere acknowledged: Frank Churchill, in suggesting a ball at the Crown (chapter 24) asks, 'Why had not Miss Woodhouse revived the former good old days of the room? She who could do anything in Highbury!' We have no doubt that he is right, just as Mr Weston's objection to the idea of her leaving a party early because it would give offence (chapter 25) is valid. Mr Knightley also takes his obligations seriously. In fact, while the local church is presented as lacking moral authority, Austen shows the responsibility for establishing values devolving on landowners like Emma and Mr Knightley. Thus their union appears appropriate long before it is in any way hinted at. The moral approbation given to the solid yeomanry in the person of Robert Martin, is also a part of this picture.

The outstanding male example of someone outside this structured society is Frank Churchill. Unlike Mr John Knightley, he has no profession, and his position with regards to property is somewhat uncertain, dependent on a capricious elderly lady. His link with his own father is tenuous, and his lack of feeling in delaying coming to pay his respects to his new 'mother-in-law' (stepmother) is regarded by Mr Knightley (our and Emma's mentor) as evidence that he is probably 'proud, luxurious and selfish' (chapter 18). It may be that some censure is implied towards Mr Weston for allowing his in-laws to bring up Frank ('some scruples and some reluctance the widower-father may be supposed to have felt' — chapter 2), but Frank's failure to take the independence which might be expected of a young man is chided by Emma as well as by Mr Knightley (chapters 14 and 18 respectively). His behaviour when he does come to Highbury is characterised by triviality and secrecy, and could be seen as subversive of the standards of that society and therefore also of wider society. It is not until near the end, almost in spite of himself, that he is given the opportunity to redeem himself, with a wife who after her brief lapse can be trusted to maintain traditional standards.

The major failing of Frank's relationship with Jane has been the secret engagement, and this is of considerable significance. It recalls the threat which, up to about a century before this period, had been posed by secret marriages. Engagement to marry should be a public act, showing as it does the acceptance of a certain place within the social structure, and demanding proper behaviour both *from* the parties involved and *to* them. While the idea of a love-match has become possible in the early nineteenth century, marriage itself is still a public transaction, involving aspects of property and inheritance (we recall Emma's fears about 'little Henry' losing his rights, chapter 26 and elsewhere). Actions like Frank's, and to a lesser extent Jane's, threaten the very fabric of society. I think we misread Austen's novels sometimes because our twentieth-century view of marriage is a far more private one, a relationship simply between individuals, even if this is normally ratified by parental and public presence at the ceremony. The very idea of a marriage settlement dealing with property is quite foreign to us today. Austen's concern with appropriate unions is integral to her views about the stability of society. Hence the satisfaction felt by the nineteenth-century reader at Emma's union with Mr Knightley would not have been purely at the personal level, but also at the rightness of concordance between Hartfield and Donwell.

Harriet Smith's situation, while reinforcing the theme of appropriate union, also emphasises the need for a woman to be set clearly within the social strata. Hence, perhaps, one of the chief evils of illegitimacy; no slur seems to be placed against her unknown parents for sexual immorality, but the vulnerability of Harriet's situation amply demonstrates the wrongness of their irresponsible behaviour.

The Harriet theme also provides an effective means of focusing on Emma's inadequacy for her role in society because her own self-will has prevented her from being properly educated. Clearly Miss Taylor has been no match for Emma; she was: 'one ... who had such an affection for her as could never find fault' (chapter 1). Undoubtedly she has given Emma much, but Emma has not learned all that she should, either in terms of accomplishment, or, what is more important, about relationships. Her blunder about Harriet and Mr Elton reveals this. There is serious doubt as to whether Miss Taylor could ever have been a totally satisfactory governess for someone like Emma. The responsibility here obviously lies with the amusingly useless Mr Woodhouse, but the humour of Austen's portrayal should not blind us to her criticism of his failure to fulfil the kind of role in society appropriate to his position as a chief landowner. The main target here, however, I would suggest, is society's failure to cope properly with the education of women, a theme reinforced near the end with the explicit mention of the responsibility for the education of young Anna Weston (chapter 53).

Much attention is given in this novel to the role of governesses, and Austen's strongest language is used to remind us of the lowly position of those entrusted with the responsibility for the education of those women who, as wives, were to have influence on their husbands' estates and on their own children's education. Governesses would also 'educate' the young boys before they went on to better qualified male care. Jane Fairfax says:

> I was not thinking of the slave-trade ... governess-trade, I assure you was all that I had in view; widely different, certainly,

as to the guilt of those who carry it on; but as to the greater misery of the victims, I do not know where it lies.

(chapter 35)

The comparison here is particularly significant, given the involvement of prominent Christians such as Wilberforce in the abolition of the slave-trade. Is Austen implying that the Christian conscience should also be aware of the oppression of victims closer to home? Even the names chosen for Mrs Elton's associates seem to support the idea of oppression: Mrs Suckling (a hint of predatoriness here, surely, as well as the implied reference to young offspring?), Mrs Bragge and Mrs Smallridge (implying small mind, petty, perhaps).

The very word 'governess' seems to be almost taboo as applied to Mrs Weston (chapter 24) and the statement of Mrs Elton, 'She was your governess, I think?' (chapter 32), is an indicator of her bad taste and ill breeding. Clearly underlings like governesses could scarcely be expected to provide a good education, not only in accomplishments and manners (even in these, few pupils would be lucky enough to find someone as qualified as Miss Fairfax), but also in discernment and academic subjects. The real education which Emma needs has always come from conversation with Mr Knightley, bereft as she is of the like from her own father. The modern reader is seldom totally happy with Mr Knightley's admonitions, and is probably glad that he is not quite omniscient and can admit to some degree of error about Jane, but even so, he is a means of allowing Emma to grow to suit her role in society. Even the best of governesses could not do this for her, and it is not suggested that schools would provide anything better. Miss Goddard's establishment, based on wholesome food and the commercial value of 'a reasonable quantity of accomplishments . . . sold at a reasonable price where . . . girls might scramble themselves into a little education without any danger of coming back prodigies' (chapter 3) reflects the values of a society where the only significance of a girl's education is the effect on her value in the marriage market.

The only explicit criticism of the limitation placed on women's role by society is in Emma's vision of herself at forty or fifty given to Harriet, when she claims that she will not marry (chapter 10). She portrays herself as having 'woman's usual occupations of eye and hand and mind . . . open to me then as they are now'. The lack of scope this suggests for Emma's talents brings home to us Austen's own potential situation, had she not by her writing put herself into the position of making an active criticism of her society. For most unmarried women, as indeed for many married ones, there will be no opportunity comparable to those she provides to her heroines. They will not have the scope for action derived from union with a man aware of his responsibilities, both to society and to himself, such as Mr Knightley here, or Captain Wentworth in *Persuasion*, Mr Darcy in *Pride and Prejudice* or the committed clergyman Edmund Bertram in *Mansfield Park*. The extent of the 'education in feeling' which the women have contributed to their spouses in the last three instances is also worth note. The horizons of many of Austen's contemporaries will, by contrast, be no wider than those of Miss Bates, but they may well lack her affability. There seems little doubt that the novelist's criticism of society, in the areas of education and its view of women's role, is not confined to the narrow world which she portrays directly.

In a few instances, Austen makes us aware of another world outside the concerns of Highbury. Light is thrown on contemporary attitudes to health and medicine, when the valetudinarianism of Mr Woodhouse and his dependence on Perry encounters his daughter Isabella's reliance on Wingfield. This enables the author to air issues about sea-bathing and the proper choice of resort, the respective virtues of Southend and Cromer allowing mention of the cost of transport (chapter 12). Austen's ironic distancing of such issues means that we are led to judge fashion from the perspective of common sense, a stance which recalls the portrayal of life at Bath in novels such as *Northanger Abbey*. The vexed question of whether Perry is going to 'set up' his carriage (chapter 41) indicates the increasing prestige of the medical profession. Even within the backwater of Highbury, changes have occurred, reflecting the commercial development of the period. The prominent place given to Ford's, 'the shop that everybody attends every day of their lives', as Frank Churchill describes it (chapter 24), shows how much provincial society has interconnections with the rise of industry.

Gloves in 'sleek, well-tied parcels of "Men's Beavers" and "York Tan"' are displayed on the counter; the provenance of such (for those days) mass-produced articles reveals a degree of central-isation of trade and manufacture. Proximity to London encour-ages some people to look outside the community for services, reminding us that the drift to the towns which featured in this period was well underway: Frank's insistence on his London hairdresser is a credible excuse when he goes to order the piano (and the speed of delivery from Broadwoods would be enviable today!) (chapters 25 and 26).

Generally speaking, however, the characters in *Emma* are relatively unaffected by the increasing social changes of the period. Even the incident when Harriet is attacked by gipsies (chapter 39) is not presented as imaging any wider tendency to disorder, though such a thing has never happened locally before. Its significance seems solely directed towards plot, involving Frank Churchill with the Harriet theme, and not, as would be the case with some writers, to convey directly the message that the tranquillity of Highbury is threatened. Nevertheless, its effect cannot be ignored within an England where the immense rise in the price of wheat resulting from the Napoleonic Wars had led to considerable hardships for the poor. The fall in prices subsequent on the return of peace led to ruin for some farmers and the enactment of the Corn Law in 1815; for Austen's contemporaries such events would be the background against which this incident was read. The situation of old John Abdy, whose son 'even though he is very well-to-do himself . . . being head man at the Crown . . . cannot keep his father without some help' (chapter 44) also throws light on the plight of those below the level of prosperity of the central characters. Again, its effect on the nineteenth-century reader would be greater than on us.

This relative detachment from the changes in transport and commerce, of which she describes the effects, and even from situ-ations and hardship, does not however obtain in Austen's treat-ment of the Church. The depiction of Mr Elton seems to me to work at two levels, that of the plot, particularly in relation to the Harriet theme, and that of social criticism presented by an author far from satisfied by what she saw of contemporary Anglicanism. We are never allowed to forget, or forgive, the discrepancy between Mr Elton's personal qualities and his official capacity. We never have any hint of his being motivated by Christian feelings, nor of his behaviour as being anything other than selfish. In his initial courting of Emma he is as blind as she is; while she misinterprets his advances as being made to Harriet, he fails to understand her response. He can be seen therefore as being as inadequate in his education as she is, with no real excuse: 'the very want of such equality [of talent and elegancy of mind] might prevent his perception of it' (chapter 16). While Emma's judgement partly reflects her own consciousness of rank, her summing him up as 'proud, assuming, conceited; very full of his own claims, and little concerned about the feelings of others' (ibid.) is borne out by his actions before and afterwards. His failure to show compassion to Harriet at the ball (chapter 38) amply demonstrates his lack of feeling, and is also marked by his complicity with his wife: 'smiles of high glee passed between him and his wife'. His unsuitability for his sacred calling is in fact evidenced by his choice of wife, for his social climbing and search for economic prosperity even when accompanied by a dearth of other good qualities, are used by Austen to indicate his personal lack of worth. In several of her novels (*Persuasion* and *Mansfield Park*, for instance) men of worth are temporarily attracted to women whose moral or mental qualities are beneath them, but they speedily become conscious of their mistake; here, by contrast, his wife's characteristics serve to bring out parallel ones latent in Mr Elton himself. Her inordinate pride in her brother-in-law's property, Maple Grove (chapter 32), her contemptuous dismissal of Highbury society ('In the course of the spring she must return their civilities by one very superior party' — chapter 34), her seizing on Jane Fairfax as proper prey for her desire to show off the social importance of her own connections (chapter 35), these and many other incidents all lead us to form a harsher judgement on her husband. Thus, what she reveals of her attitude to the calls his parish makes upon him is both in character for her and a presumed reflection of his own contempt for the people to whom he should be ministering:

> He really is engaged from morning to night. There is no end of people's coming to him, on some pretence or other. The magis-

trates, and overseers, and churchwardens, are always wanting his opinion. They seem not able to do anything without him . . .

(chapter 52)

She goes on to state, 'this is the most troublesome parish that ever was'. When her husband arrives, we are presented with a discrepancy between the regard in which Mrs Elton claims that Mr Knightley holds her husband, and the fact that no message has been left for Mr Elton. We deduce that not only does he hold his parish duties in small account, he also fails to perform them properly.

Much earlier (chapter 10) we have seen the nature of his charity to the poor. Emma and Harriet have been ministering to the poor, a point at which we see another side of Emma:

> She understood their ways, could allow for their ignorance and their temptations, had no romantic expectations of extraordinary virtue from those, for whom education had done so little; entered into their troubles with ready sympathy, and always gave her assistance with as much intelligence as good-will.

Even so, she is uncertain as to the lasting effects of these scenes of wretchedness — a proper scepticism, for when the young ladies meet Mr Elton they are immediately more interested in his supposed love for Harriet. His active compassion is clearly much less than theirs:

> The wants and sufferings of the poor family, however, were the first subject on meeting. He had been going to call on them. His visit he would now defer.

It seems to me that Austen is suggesting to the reader a serious degree of doubt as to how far, if at all, Mr Elton will have the same degree of compassion for the poor as that displayed by Emma and Harriet. We are left to wonder if he had indeed been planning to visit the poor people, or whether he felt this claim would help make him attractive to Emma. Certainly we have doubts as to the quality of the judgement Harriet voices soon after the truth about Mr Elton's feelings has been divulged: 'Mr Elton is so good to the poor' (chapter 19). It appears to be as ill founded as her other delusions about his good qualities. There is little evidence of any interest in anyone other than himself;

his reference to John Abdy (chapter 44; see page 15 above) in conversation with Miss Bates seems to have been merely in order to show how well informed he was about Frank Churchill's movements (unlike Miss Bates's own reaction of concern). His irritation about the apparent needs of Mr Knightley's servant, 'I have nothing to do with William's wants' (chapter 52), is in close proximity to his wife's strictures on the Donwell retainers 'who are all extremely awkward and remiss', so that no suggestion of pastoral care is conveyed.

It could be argued that Austen's depiction of the Eltons is a mere literary device, no more than a use of contrast to make them a foil for the positive qualities of her central pair, Emma and Mr Knightley. The contrast is certainly there, very notably as the difference is conveyed between Emma's practical charity and Mrs Elton's self-indulgent use of patronage, between Mr Elton's lack of concern either for the people in his flock or for parish affairs and Mr Knightley's competent involvement with both. But these very elements of contrast are integrally related to Mr Elton's profession, which we are never allowed to forget. Even at the end, when we are told of the marriage ceremonies, we cannot ignore Mr Elton's being 'called on ... to join the hands of Mr Knightley and Miss Woodhouse,' as well as the collusion between the Eltons in scorning the meanness of the occasion (chapter 55). They are, in fact, the only characters in the novel with whom we are not allowed to have any sympathy at all. Surely it is no accident that this severe negative judgement is made against the representative of a Church which Austen often seems to find lacking the level of Christian practice which she as a committed Christian demands.

In reading the novel in this light, I would not go so far as to see Highbury totally as a metaphor for the state of England at the time, but its society is certainly a microcosm of English society, in which the Church could be seen as often neglecting its function of upholding values which were needed more than ever in this period of threat. If the Church left a moral vacuum, especially in its concern for the people, as it did in Highbury, the duty devolved on those who, like Emma, had birth and possessions, and, like Mr Knightley, a great estate (chapter 16). This responsibility on those with property is a concept so alien to us today that we are perhaps blinded to this part of Austen's message about the 'larger world'. She has a great deal to say which has implications far beyond the miniature portrait of 'three or four families in a country village' which she describes as 'the very thing to work on'. From a superb ironist we should perhaps hesitate to accept so apparently modest a disclaimer. While *Emma* answers to this description it also succeeds in presenting an indictment of some of the ills of contemporary society. The *nouveaux-riches* were vulgar and uncaring and showed no sign of taking on the obligations of their position, or caring properly for tenants and dependants. Too little attention was being given to education, particularly that of women, whose position as guardians of the affective values of society and inculcation of them into the young was being eroded, their educators being the despised governesses whose own position was little better than of slaves. Many women with the potential to give much were offered no better role than triviality and idleness. The Church, ideally the custodian of value, was neglecting its task. Salvation could come only from those whose concern with their own property gave them a proper sense of responsibility, both for those under them and for the wider world. It is by no means fanciful to see *Emma* as conveying important truths about a 'wider world' about which Jane Austen not only knows but also makes judgements. Had her art been as miniature as the critic's words suggest, it is doubtful if it could have maintained reader interest past the great changes of the Victorian period and into our own totally dissimilar age!

AFTERTHOUGHTS

1

Should we regard Mr Knightley as 'our and Emma's mentor' (page 11)?

2

'Engagement to marry should be a public act' (page 11). Do you agree?

3

How does this essay seek to demonstrate its claim that Highbury 'is certainly a microcosm of English society' (page 18)?

4

Compare this essay with the essay by Watts on pages 116–123. What different approaches have the authors taken?

Kathleen Parkinson

Kathleen Parkinson is Principal Lecturer in English at the Roehampton Institute of Higher Education, and author of Penguin Masterstudies *on* The Great Gatsby *and* Tender is the Night.

ESSAY

Courtship and marriage in *Emma*

... something so like perfect happiness that it could bear no other name.

(chapter 49)

Courtship plays a major role in *Emma* but marriage constitutes its central theme. Whereas the former is almost invariably treated as a source of comedy, marriage is revealed as a subject of serious consideration. However, in literature, as in life, the two activities are intimately related and an examination of some of the ways in which Austen focuses on courtship highlights many of the values the novelist attaches to matrimony.

It is perhaps as well to begin by stressing that Austen analyses the nature of marriage in both social and personal contexts. The marriage vows constitute a public *contract* which is crucial in determining such vital matters as inheritance and status. They also announce a personal union offering individuals the chance to discover their greatest happiness and fulfilment. This double perspective is maintained largely through our perception of the progress which Emma Woodhouse, the self-styled 'imaginist' (chapter 39), makes in understanding for herself the issues involved.

She begins the novel half in love with the conventions of romantic behaviour. But the failure of her various attempts at matchmaking leads her to question the codes which have informed her views. This can be seen most clearly in her attitude towards the language of courtship. She begins by admiring the linguistic extravagances of her various 'admirers', yet eventually recognises that the conventions of courtly love not only encourage artifice and dissimulation but trivialise a woman's identity by providing her with a model that is insipid and passive. By learning to value language as a means of confronting real experience, Emma achieves a relationship in which 'tell[ing] truths' (chapter 43) in a plain unequivocal way assures her a role as a rational, intelligent, morally aware woman and wife.

Weddings provide a frame for the narrative, which begins on the wedding day of 'poor Miss Taylor' (chapter 1), takes a new direction with the advent of Mrs Elton, the triumphant 'bride' who is determined to extract the maximum prestige from her 'interesting situation' (chapter 22), and ends with the successful matches of the three central couples. The closing words indeed promise a life of personal fulfilment for Emma and Mr Knightley in 'the perfect happiness of the union'.

The brief outline of Mr Weston's marital experiences in chapter 2 offers an introduction to many of the financial and social issues relating to matrimony which have a place in the novel. For example, the reader is informed that he is now in a position to marry 'a woman as portionless even as Miss Taylor'. A portion, or dowry, was the money a bride brought to the marriage, which then become her husband's property. Marriage could thus be a very mercantile and competitive matter, particularly as the wife's lack of any legal right to her own possessions could make it a valuable form of investment for impecunious bachelors or families with a son to be set up in life. Austen makes this a central theme in her earlier novel, *Sense and Sensibility*. From the woman's point of view, as divorce was virtually impossible, choice of a partner was a vital matter, and it was not until the Married Women's Property Act of 1882 that women gained some measure of control over their lives. These matters are not of immediate relevance in the case of *Emma*, but they form the context of women's expectations of marriage.

Suffice it to say that Emma was secure in the knowledge of a large endowment; Mrs Elton made the most of her more modest one on the marriage market; money was forthcoming for Harriet; Jane Fairfax had nothing.

Mr Weston possesses 'an easy competence', and his freedom of action is commented on: 'He had made his fortune, bought his house, and obtained his wife'; he is at liberty to seek happiness with a 'well-judging and truly amiable woman'. Even more revealing is the authorial comment: 'He had only himself to please in his choice: his fortune was his own'. Such terseness on the part of the author may imply some criticism of Mr Weston, or it may simply convey that as a middle-aged man he can suit himself rather than his family. By contrast, in his previous marriage his wife's moral instability, their personal incompatibility, the lack of an assured financial position, the disparity of their social status, the question of property and unfavourable family attitudes had all contributed to its failure.

These same problems beset the other courtships, but they are all finally resolved. Emma, for instance, warns Harriet that a young man like Robert Martin who was 'not born to an independence' (chapter 4) should not marry before he is thirty. However, we are left in no doubt that Emma has a tendency to make categorical statements based on very little evidence and also to tailor her arguments to her own wishes. Her assertion that, as Martin's wife, Harriet would be cut off from the benefits of contact with Hartfield is expressed in terms which grate upon the modern reader, though it may have some justification. However, as an upwardly mobile farmer, Robert Martin is welcome at other Highbury houses and also at the John Knightleys in Brunswick Square. Emma's rejection of the idea of a match between Jane Fairfax and Mr Knightley on the grounds of her nephew Henry's prospects (chapter 26) receives short shrift when her own position as mistress of Donwell Abbey is assured. Frank Churchill's dependence on the power wielded by his capricious aunt ensures that Jane would never be acceptable at Enscombe. He certainly is not the man to make a romantic sacrifice of all for love, whatever Emma might judge initially. However, while acknowledging these issues, Austen dispatches Mrs Churchill swiftly in order to remove this particular obstacle. Those who exploit the power of wealth and status receive little sympathy from her. Austen is far more concerned with personal compatibility — which may mean social compatibility too, but only as this reflects education and upbringing — intelligence, and, above all, moral awareness. Emma loves to talk of marriage prospects, particularly Harriet's, in terms of an 'alliance', a word denoting contracts between families, but she learns that there are other values to be considered too. However, although Austen questions the notion of the supremacy of class and property in a union, she does not reject these: Harriet does not marry outside her social sphere; Jane Fairfax is suited to Enscombe by virtue of her birth as well as her personal endowments of looks and intelligence; above all, the estates of Hartfield and Donwell Abbey are united in the love match of Emma and Mr Knightley, whose emotional alliance validates their property alliance.

When Mrs Weston and Mr Knightley wonder what will become of Emma (chapter 5), naturally enough they refer to her falling in love and marrying. For middle-class women there was no alternative, other than putting their intellects up for sale as governesses or living as old maids, the state so dreaded by Harriet. The status of the wife in civil law was promulgated by a prominent lawyer in 1758:

> ... the husband and wife are one person in law; that is, the very being or legal existence of the woman is suspended during the marriage or at least is incorporated and consolidated into that of the husband; under whose wing, protection and cover she performs everything.
> (quoted in the Introduction to Mary Wollstonecraft, *Vindications of the Rights of Women*, ed. M R Kramnick (Harmondsworth, 1985), p. 34)

Such a conception of matrimony is deftly suggested in the lives of Mrs Weston and Isabella, who identify themselves totally in the figure of submissive — and in Isabella's case mindless — wife and devoted mother. The comment that Mrs Weston, 'like a sweet-tempered woman and a good wife' (chapter 29), modifies her judgement about the Crown Inn expresses gentle irony on the author's part; so too does the observation that Isabella was always so 'innocently busy' that she 'might have been a model of right feminine happiness' (chapter 17). Fortunately, Emma does not choose such models for her own marital happiness.

The ideal union founded on mutual respect for each other's sensitivity, judgement, intelligence and integrity is attained by Emma and Mr Knightley. In the case of the Harriet Smith–Robert Martin and Jane Fairfax–Frank Churchill matches, Mr Knightley judges that the more stable and principled partner will influence the other for good. The two principal lovers know their union is based on equality and honesty. Mr Knightley is confident of 'the beauty of truth and sincerity in all our dealings with each other' (chapter 51). He does not know about poor deluded Harriet's feelings, but otherwise he is justified. As regards their social or financial equality, although he may pronounce the traditional view that 'A man would always wish to give a woman a better home than the one he takes her from' (chapter 49), this is not applicable in their case. Just before this, when Emma tries to imagine Harriet as 'the dearest, the friend, the wife to whom he looked for all the best blessings of existence' (chapter 48), her sudden realisation that this is the position she ardently covets for herself underlines her view of a wife's positive role. Although Mr Knightley has long been the judicious father-figure, the mentor who was otherwise lacking in her life, he became so precisely because he recognised her potential. Now, when he declares himself, he says that loving her has enriched his life. He is prepared to modify his judgement of Frank Churchill and Harriet in accord with hers, thus allowing her to be a mentor too. Yet, though Austen conveys that this is an ideal passion by such phrases as 'the happiest dream' (chapter 49) and 'something so like perfect happiness' (ibid.), she deliberately controls the emotion by her light ironic tone:

> What did she say? Just what she ought, of course. A lady always does.
>
> (ibid.)
>
> The wedding was very much like other weddings . . .
>
> (chapter 55)

Some time before the two reach this happy resolution there is, in chapter 8, a quarrel between them which highlights some of the problems of relations between the sexes. Emma is half on the defensive, half eager to attack, partly ready to concede that his views are worthy of respect, partly flirtatious. It is really a stage in their unacknowledged courtship, though neither recognises it as such. When she claims that pretty doll-like Harriet is what every man wants, and even dares to suggest that she is the girl for him if he should ever think of marrying, Emma is challenging him in the battle of the sexes. In the event, she comes close to tempting providence. Yet she is also making a valid point: a girl is judged by her looks and men frequently do chose a pretty face regardless of the empty mind it conceals. One of Austen's earlier heroines ponders this phenomenon in *Sense and Sensibility*: '[Mr Palmer's] temper might perhaps be a little soured by finding, like many others of his sex, that through some unaccountable bias in favour of beauty, he was the husband of a very silly woman' (chapter 20). Men choose, women wait to be chosen: 'A man always imagines a woman to be ready for anybody who asks her' (chapter 8). But when she urges that Robert Martin's looks and manners are disagreeable to women, she tells herself it is a woman's privilege to pronounce on these matters. What she does not realise is that she is endorsing the stereotypical image of women as having no other function than to be custodians of the frivolous and trivial. Mary Wollstonecraft, an older contemporary of Austen, who had shocked public opinion by her ideas and way of life, explained why women accepted so limited a view of themselves:

> Men have various employments and pursuits which engage their attention, and give character to the opening mind; but women, confined to [the idea that beauty is a woman's sceptre] and having their thoughts constantly directed to the most insignificant part of themselves, seldom extend their views
>
> (op. cit., p.131)

Mr Knightley robustly refutes Emma's charges by pointing out that intelligent men do not want silly wives, but later he mentions another motivation by disclosing that Mr Elton, darling of the Highbury ladies, reveals a different side of himself to men. There exists a man's world from which women are excluded, and here Mr Elton talks enthusiastically of some young ladies possessing twenty thousand pounds a piece. If the implication is that Mr Elton is not a 'man of sense', then it certainly proves to be fully justified. It is significant that Austen handles his successful courtship and marriage retrospectively and with dispatch: his 'vanity and prudence were equally contented' (chapter 22).

In a leisured, aristocratic society in which form and style are all-important, conduct is likely to be rigidly dictated by convention and ritual, particularly where relations between the sexes are concerned. 'Lover', in its use in this novel, defines the man who declares his honourable intentions and whose formal courtship is a prelude to marriage.

Austen's treatment of the courtships is complex. Some exist as fantasies of Emma's shaping which escape her control when the characters in her contrived scenarios, Mr Elton, Harriet and Frank Churchill, prove to have their own designs; the trouble is, her schemes ignore the patent evidence of their real inclinations. Other courtships are hinted at or hoped for or feared in village gossip. Others are concealed or unacknowledged. They develop through a series of comic mistakes or blunders which help to establish the tone of the novel. The word 'blunder' recurs, being finally recalled by Frank Churchill as he gazes at his beloved and comments that she can smile now that 'the whole blunder is spread before her' (chapter 54). The same might well be said of Emma and Mr Knightley or Harriet and Robert Martin.

Their courtships are differentiated through the style and language of the narrative, as well as by the way the suitors write or speak, and the conversational, literary or epistolary merits of the men are frequently a subject of discussion. Austen, however, discriminates between the language of 'gallantry' (always a suspect word in *Emma*) and that of sincere feeling: the former is artificial or duplicitous, while the latter attempts to match words to the perceived truth; the one, while appearing to distinguish a woman, in fact reduces her to a vacuous object, but the other accepts her as a rational being who shares a common language with men. Mr Knightley, indeed, affirms that he lacks the required eloquence of the lover: 'I cannot make speeches, Emma ... If I loved you less I might be able to talk about it more ... I have been a very indifferent lover' (chapter 49).

While Mr Knightley's characteristic style of speaking is sometimes a subject for comedy, it is also presented as a model of the conjunction of truth and sincere feeling. When he proposes to Emma, the author comments:

> The subject followed; it was in plain, unaffected gentleman-like English, such as Mr Knightley used *even* to the woman he was in love with . . .
>
> (chapter 51 — author's italics)

The modifying force of 'even' highlights this as uncommon. His style of speaking distinguishes him from Mr Elton and Frank Churchill, though not, significantly, from the despised Robert Martin, whose letter of proposal to Harriet Emma has to acknowledge as excellent:

> . . . as a composition it would not have disgraced a gentleman; the language, though plain, was strong and unaffected . . . [It] expressed good sense, warm attachment, liberality, propriety, even delicacy of feeling.
>
> (chapter 7)

These are virtues indeed, and ones which Emma will learn to value in her own case. Her recognition of the merits of his style measures the extent to which she represses her own discriminating intelligence in favour of wilful fantasies about love. She is fully aware of the fatuity of Harriet's final dismissal of the letter as 'but a short one too' (chapter 7), though she fails to acknowledge her own responsibility for Harriet's opinions.

The virtues that Emma nominates in Robert Martin's letter are all those traditionally associated with the age of chivalry. In Chaucer's Knight and Squire, for instance, they represent the summit of the knightly code of honour, and, indeed, Mr Knightley's name embodies this. However, Austen often updates this image as far as male attitudes towards women are concerned. While chivalrous young men in the fourteenth century were required to be adept at the language of courtly love, in her view the nineteenth-century gentleman expressed his chivalry best by addressing a woman as a rational being. Although Austen makes all the suitors engage in quests or acts attributable to the traditional lover as knight errant, she does so for comic effect. Robert Martin goes three miles out of his way to find walnuts for Harriet, though he fails in Emma's estimation by forgetting to buy the novel his beloved has praised. But, significantly, in

Ford's he rejects any sign of the despised lover's rancour, being far more concerned about her feelings. Mr Elton, his 'gallantry' always on the alert, begs the commission of getting Harriet's portrait framed in London, and is heard to talk effusively about his 'exceedingly precious' (chapter 8) burden. Frank Churchill too goes on a mission, ostensibly to get his hair cut, but in fact to buy his beloved a piano as an 'offering of love' (chapter 26). Naturally, the real burden of his impulsive act falls on Jane Fairfax. He also saves a maiden in distress by rescuing Harriet from the gipsies, an escapade which Austen uses to heighten the comic misunderstandings, since it allows Emma to indulge in further misguided matchmaking. Mr Knightley's acts of chivalry, however, reveal a true delicacy of feeling: he goes out of his way to help a tedious old maid, and he dances with Harriet out of a sympathetic appreciation of what a girl must feel when she is publicly snubbed, another act which has ironic consequences as it raises Harriet's hopes. Although they are exploited for their comic potential by the author, these acts of chivalry reflect a range of male attitudes towards women; they also portray effectively the psychology and moral sensitivity — or lack of it — of the men in question.

Mr Elton's courtship, for example, reveals his lack of true gentility, whatever Emma might at first profess to Harriet. She knows his determination 'to sigh and languish, and study for compliments' (chapter 66) is pure affectation, and would be intolerable if directed towards herself. She goes so far as to admit to herself that he is 'almost too gallant' (ibid.) to be really in love, and she sees that his fulsome praises of the portrait reveal a total lack of discrimination. Yet she persuades herself that he speaks with 'a sort of sighing animation, which had a vast deal of the lover' (ibid.), for 'anything less would certainly have been too little in a lover' (ibid.). Austen's choice of language manages to convey very deftly how fatuously the clergyman adheres to the model of romantic behaviour, at the same time as it measures the extent of Emma's self-deception. She is perfectly happy to accept his posturings on Harriet's behalf.

During the episode of Harriet's collection of riddles, which gives a good indication of the level of her taste and education, Emma notices his care that 'nothing ungallant, nothing that did not breathe a compliment to the sex [i.e. women] should pass his lips' (chapter 9). His own contribution is devoid of real feeling and fulsome in its adulation. For the rest, his poem presents the conventional encomium of 'woman, lovely woman' (ibid.) as queen who reduces the master of the universe to servility. Emma chooses to regard this as 'a very proper compliment' (ibid.) to Harriet, the expression of 'an attachment which a woman may well feel pride in creating'. One wonders whose creative power she is delighting in here! Mary Wollstonecraft, in the work already cited, angrily dismisses 'those pretty feminine phrases which the men condescendingly use to soften [women's] slavish dependence' (op. cit., p.82). Austen ridicules them. When, true to the convention, Mr Elton declares himself 'ready to die if she refused him' (chapter 15), Emma has had enough, and employs a plain, brusque style to dismiss him.

Despite this débâcle, she is ready to build another fantasy around the figure of the 'lover', this time in the person of Frank Churchill. Even though she sees through his 'gallantry' (chapter 29) towards herself, she is delighted to regard him as 'the hero of the evening' (ibid.), and to misinterpret his parting sigh. 'It was natural for him to feel that he had *cause* to sigh . . . He was more in love with her than Emma had supposed' (chapter 30). She sustains these fantasies of her power by rejecting him in her imagination, though she is acute enough to allow that she is no heroine of romantic fiction herself, for the word 'sacrifice' has no place in her terms of dismissal. Austen later widens the gap between romantic fantasy and genuine feeling by re-introducing the concept of sacrifice. Upon grasping that Mr Knightley loves herself, Emma quickly rejects that 'heroism of sentiment' and 'simple sublimity' (chapter 49) of giving him up for her friend's sake that the convention demanded. When Mr Knightley offers to make his home at Hartfield, she recognises that this is a *real* sacrifice of 'a great deal of independence' (chapter 51) on his part.

Frank Churchill is more than ready to be gallant to Emma, partly as a cover for his attachment to Jane but also because he enjoys a light-hearted flirtation with a pretty, vivacious girl. Early in their acquaintance he promises, 'I will speak the truth, and nothing suits me so well' (chapter 24). He is true to his promise: he does indeed tell no lies and his style of speech becomes him while at the same time it suits his purpose of carrying on his private love affair with Jane. He makes the most of the ambivalent relation of language to truth, and his equivocal use of it during, for example, their discusssion of the supposed illicit love between Jane and her closest friend's husband tempts Emma into transgressing in 'the duty of woman by woman' (chapter 27) on several occasions. At Box Hill she is still ready to play what she conceives to be his game, but she no longer enjoys it. His announcement that Miss Woodhouse, 'who, wherever she is, presides' (chapter 43), has ordered him to speak, mockingly elevates her to the same kind of power as Mr Elton's poem had done, but in reality it does her no service. That the concealed engagement of Frank Churchill and Jane Fairfax increasingly interacts with the tensions and unacknowledged feelings of the others, conveys Austen's view of the moral uncertainties of a secret courtship.

As the lover of Jane, yet the ostensible admirer of Emma, Frank Churchill plays a morally problematic role. The secrecy surrounding his engagement to Jane highlights his tendency to suit himself in all his relationships. As the mysterious, controlling figure in Jane's life, he ignores her moral sensibility and vulnerable position during what she, in a moment of anger, terms their 'hasty and imprudent attachment' (chapter 43). His game of innuendo and ambiguity with Emma is interpreted as courtship and might have caused pain to all the women involved. Mr Knightley — admittedly no unbiased judge — criticises him for 'manoeuvring and finessing' (chapter 18), and Jane later owns to never having known 'the blessing of one tranquil hour' (chapter 48). The full irony of Emma's flirtation with Frank Churchill is apparent to her only when she is forced to concede that Harriet's interpretation of Mr Knightley's behaviour may be justified:

> Harriet, I will only venture to declare, that Mr Knightley is the last man in the world, who would intentionally give any woman the idea of his feeling for her more than he really does.
>
> (chapter 47)

Emma is understandably critical of Frank Churchill when the story of his engagement comes to light, and her first comment includes sympathy for Jane: 'What right had he to come among us with affection and faith engaged, and with manners so *very* disengaged?' (chapter 46). Her play on words is terse and controlled in her discrimination between 'affections' and 'faith' on the one hand, and 'manners' on the other. She employs verbal skill to make an ethical point rejecting mere form in favour of sensitivity, feeling and honour. Jane Fairfax has the last word on her lover's verbal manipulation of the truth when she smilingly accuses him of courting reminders of their former troubles. She too can match his linguistic dexterity, but, like Emma, she uses it to serious effect: she knows that for a personality such as his, courting exposure was part of the game of courting herself. For Emma the game is over: style is only of service in so far as it represents real values.

By means of the comedy surrounding courtship in *Emma* Austen explores some of the conventions governing relations between the sexes which have shaped a woman's self-image as girl and wife. However, the novel ends with a union which represents more than the traditional happy ending of comedy, for it is one which endorses certain social values when these are allied with moral awareness and personal integrity.

AFTERTHOUGHTS

What do you understand by 'the conventions of romantic behaviour' (page 22)?

Explain the significance of the reference to the Married Women's Property Act of 1882 (page 22).

Do you agree that Emma and Mr Knightley share a 'love match' (page 24)?

What are the social values that *Emma* 'endorses' (see last paragraph)?

Susie Campbell

Susie Campbell teaches at North Westminster Community School. She has written a study of Jane Eyre *for the Penguin Masterstudies series.*

ESSAY

The significance of games in *Emma*

Games feature prominently in *Emma*. The inhabitants of Highbury are keen games-players and they enjoy a variety of games, including backgammon, whist and piquet. Backgammon, Mr Woodhouse's particular favourite, is a board-game for two players. In the very first chapter, Emma is hoping 'to get her father tolerably through the evening' by means of backgammon, although, in the event, this is made unnecessary by the arrival of Mr Knightley. Whist is a card-game, played by two players against another pair. The 'whist-club night' is an important social occasion in Highbury, so much so that Mr Perry is outraged when Mr Elton, their best player, absents himself in order to take Harriet's picture to London (chapter 8). The game of piquet is a more intimate game, involving two players and thirty-two cards. We learn that Mrs Goddard is a keen piquet player. On the evening of the Coles' party, she is engaged to play piquet with Mr Woodhouse while Emma is out. Even at the Martins' farm, games form an important part of evening entertainment. Harriet tells Emma of their 'merry evening games' (chapter 4). As well as these board- and card-games, we also learn of the word-games played by the young people of Highbury. Harriet and Emma puzzle over riddles, enigmas and conundrums, and later they are joined by Frank Churchill and Jane Fairfax for the alphabet game.

Games of various kinds, then, appear throughout *Emma*. But what is their significance? In this essay, I will try to show that Austen uses them to say something about certain aspects of Highbury society. Games in *Emma*, I suggest, function as symbols of the society in which they are played. The peculiar organisation and way of operation that is common to all the games described in this book reflect aspects of the organisation and operation of Highbury society itself. I will, therefore, begin my discussion by looking more closely at the characteristics of the games played in *Emma* and examining how they work to symbolise features of Highbury society. I will then move on to talk more specifically about *word-games* and to discuss their special role in the book.

Games such as board- and card-games are highly disciplined activities, governed by strict rules and regulations. In order to play, each player must understand and agree to abide by the rules, and accept the role assigned to him or her within the game. Whilst such games are about competition and winning, they are equally about a group or pair of people consenting to submit to a set of precise regulations. We might say that they are about establishing and maintaining *order*, the particular order of the game without which the competition and winning cannot take place. If we take chess as a more familiar example, it becomes obvious that, in order for the game to take place, each player must know and abide by the regulated moves for each piece. If each player were to decide for her or himself what moves the pieces could make, the result would be chaos and the game could not proceed. In fact, to some extent, *all* games are about rules and order, even the apparently freer kind of games, such as chase, hide and seek, or a make-believe game. (It is this kind of game that Austen is presumably referring to when she writes of how Mr Woodhouse was distressed by the 'more animated sort [of game], which Mr Weston had occasionally introduced' — chapter 41.) But even this kind of game has its own rules and discipline; rules, for example, about 'home-base', 'lives', or counting to a hundred without looking, and limits within which the characters in a make-believe game must act.

Some commentators who have written about games see the

setting up of rules and limits as *the* essential feature of play-activity. The educational psychologist Vygotsky, for example, argues that the pleasure of a game lies in choosing to submit to the rules. He says, 'The essential attribute of play is a rule that has become a desire'.[1] So, rules, limits, and finding pleasure in maintaining the game's order are crucial characteristics, especially of the very disciplined games mostly played in Highbury. Looked at in this light, the games in *Emma* begin to take on a possible new significance. To understand this, we need to look more carefully at Highbury society.

Highbury also functions by observing a strict set of rules and by maintaining a very particular order. There are a number of commonly held, unwritten 'laws' governing everyone's rank and position. It is by observing these rules that the smooth running of Highbury society is maintained. Marriages and alliances are formed on the basis of these rules. Friendships are formed within their limits. If these limits are overstepped even slightly, the strict social order of Highbury is threatened. Mr Knightley is worried by Emma's patronage of Harriet, for example, because he fears it will unsettle her and disturb the existing order. He says:

> Hartfield will only put her out of conceit with all the other places she belongs to. She will grow just refined enough to be uncomfortable with those among whom birth and circumstances have placed her home.
>
> (chapter 5)

The ball at the Crown Inn provides a good opportunity for a demonstration of the hierarchy that governs this order:

> Mr Weston and Mrs Elton led the way, Mr Frank Churchill and Miss Woodhouse followed. Emma must submit to stand second to Mrs Elton, though she had always considered the ball as peculiarly for her.
>
> (chapter 38)

These unwritten rules are never more obvious than when Mrs Elton crudely insists on their observance. On the ill-fated

---

[1] L S Vygotsky, *Mind in Society* (Harvard Massachusetts, 1978), p.99.

Box Hill trip, for instance, she is put out by Frank's attentions to Emma and asserts her right to take precedence. She is the '*Chaperon* of the party' (chapter 43), she insists, asserting her superior status as a married woman. Her husband mollifies her by assuring her that everyone understands this: 'Everyone knows what is due to *you*'. Emma herself can be just as crudely explicit about the unwritten rules that uphold the order of Highbury society. She says to Harriet:

> The yeomanry are precisely the order of people with whom I feel I can have nothing to do. A degree or two lower, and a creditable appearance might interest me; I might hope to be useful to their families in some way or other. But a farmer can need none of my help, and is therefore in one sense as much above my notice as in every other he is below it.

> (chapter 4)

The order of Highbury society, then, depends on a precise observance of a particular set of unwritten but commonly acknowledged rules. Within the limits set up by these rules, visits are made, marriage partners sought, and charity bestowed. I suggest that, by drawing our attention to the *games* played in Highbury, Austen offers us a critical picture of this kind of *social* organisation. In Highbury, people obey rules, keep to their assigned roles and 'make moves' in the right order as though they were participants in some all-encompassing game of backgammon or chess. Moreover, the Highbury 'social game' is also about competition and winning — evidenced by the rivalry between Mrs Elton and Emma, and the 'competition' over husbands between the unmarried women of the circle. Austen uses games, then, to present a satirical view of Highbury society: a critical but amusing view of it as a giant game.

But games also have other characteristics that have more serious implications for Highbury society. Games are strangely static activities. There are, of course, plenty of changes and alterations *within* a game. Players make moves, lose pieces, win tricks, but none of these permanently affect the games themselves. They remain static, unchanged by the small changes within their framework. This illuminates a significant feature of Highbury society. One of the functions of its strict maintenance of order and precedence is to minimise change. For example, Emma insists that the Coles, a family in Highbury with wealth recently acquired through trade, accommodate themselves to the existing order. She is initially outraged at the thought that they might invite her to their party and thinks that 'they ought to be taught that it is not for them to arrange the terms on which the superior families would visit them' (chapter 25). (In fact, the Coles prove themselves ready to acknowledge and respect Highbury's table of precedence and Emma graciously consents to be their guest.) This kind of inflexibility ensures that despite individual changes in fortune, there is no overall alteration to Highbury society. Whenever disturbing elements are introduced to Highbury, they are quickly neutralised or checked and the existing order is re-established. The arrival of Mrs Elton, for example, temporarily disturbs Highbury society as she displaces Emma from her position of supremacy. However, Emma's marriage to Mr Knightley soon puts her back in her old place and restores the previous order.

The keenest games player in the book is Mr Woodhouse. He likes their lack of change and their reassuring stability. This is significant, as Mr Woodhouse represents the dangers of refusing to allow change. He regards any change, even one for the better, as little short of a tragedy. Austen describes him as 'a nervous man . . . fond of every body that he was used to, and hating to part with them; hating change of every kind' (chapter 1). Marriage, 'as the origin of change', is to Mr Woodhouse a most undesirable and unhappy event. He is barely reconciled to the match between Emma and Knightley, even with Emma's assurance that 'she was not going from Hartfield; she should be always there, she was introducing no change in their numbers or their comforts but for the better' (chapter 53). Mr Woodhouse demonstrates how an insistence on permanence and immutability can be morbid, confining and unhealthy. The games that he so enjoys in turn represent the way that Highbury has organised itself similarly to resist any real change.

If we look more closely at how the stasis of games is related to their structure and organisation, we can learn more about what is happening in Highbury. Games are essentially independent or autonomous organisations. The rules and limits that govern what happens inside a game also serve to establish a boundary between the game and the outside world. Games are largely self-contained, self-governing units, detached from the everyday concerns of the world of human history and experience. From the point of view of that world, games are frivolous and trivial, irrelevant to the serious business of life. But, for the player engaged in the game, there is a clearly defined goal and point to the activity: a goal and purpose set up by the rules of the game itself and independent of the aims of the outside world.

I think that this sheds important light on the way that Highbury society sees itself. It sees itself as an independent, self-governing order. It ignores the fact that its structure is in fact determined by a set of general economic and class relations. Austen shows, for example, that social position is affected by wealth. Emma Woodhouse, for instance, owes her leading position in Highbury, in part, to her wealth. The novel begins with the words: 'Emma Woodhouse, handsome, clever, and *rich*' (author's italics). Mr Knightley also owes some of his import-ance in Highbury to his fortune. The social relations between himself and Robert Martin, for example, are partly determined by their economic relations. Theirs is not an equal friendship. Mr Knightley is Mr Martin's patron and adviser, reflecting their respective positions as estate owner and farmer. Class is an even more important factor in determining social relations. Crucially, Emma's, and even more Mr Knightley's, wealth is established, landed wealth. They are both members of the gentry class. Contrasted with them are the Coles who are 'in fortune and style of living, second only to the family at Hartfield' (chapter 25), but because their wealth has been acquired recently and through trade, they are of a different class and hold a social position far below Emma's. These economic and social relations are part of the wider social organisation of the country in general. Moreover, they are *historical* relations. That is, they have come into being through a history of development and change, and they are subject to continuing fluctuation and change.

But Highbury society seems to regard itself as detached from and independent of these wider, historical relations. It tries to maintain its order, its unwritten laws and its hierarchy as though they were chosen by Highbury alone and an end in themselves. Emma's reluctance to go to the Coles' is a case in point. The only purpose of her planned refusal is to teach them the rules of Highbury's social game, as though it were something she and the other inhabitants of Highbury had set up and could completely control. Indeed, for Emma, upholding the proper order of precedence and rank is no longer a question of usefulness or of social organisation, but of 'elegance', almost as though she regards it as having some kind of aesthetic or artistic value. She is critical of Frank Churchill's casual attitudes and thinks that 'his indifference to a confusion of rank, bordered too much on inelegance of mind' (chapter 34). She has a similar criticism to make of Mr Weston. She thinks he would be improved by more social discrimination and 'a little less of open-heartedness' (chapter 38). It is as if, for Emma at least, the middle- and upper-middle-class society of Highbury is an autonomous order whose only function is to maintain itself without change or disturbance. Even when she appears to promote Harriet's social mobility by encouraging her to think of marrying above her station, she does not wish to see any fundamental change. When she is suddenly confronted with the possibility of Harriet's marrying Mr Knightley, her outrage is partly due to her sense that she, Emma, is Mr Knightley's social equal and only she must marry him.

It is not only Emma who has this kind of attitude. The other inhabitants of Highbury equally ignore the existence of any world outside its confines. Even Frank Churchill, who moves in a circle wider than the immediate neighbourhood, is regarded as strictly Highbury property. When the Highbury community consider that it is time that he paid them a visit, they pay no heed to the possibility that he might have other obligations and connections. Austen writes:

> Now, upon his father's marriage, it was very generally proposed, as a most proper attention, that the visit should take place. There was not a dissentient voice on the subject, either when Mrs Perry drank tea with Mrs and Miss Bates, or when Mrs and Miss Bates returned to visit. Now was the time for Mr Frank Churchill to come among them . . .
>
> (chapter 2)

The humour of this passage lies in the conviction of the High-bury inhabitants that if they have agreed upon something, it must be so.

The reason for Highbury's insistence on its own all-encompassing importance and its detachment from a wider world of general upheaval and change may be that it can then delude itself that it is a permanent order that will never change. Austen's novels have often been read as though they celebrate the idea of permanence and stability. In the Introduction to the Longman Study Texts edition of *Emma*, for example, Paul Cheetham points out that Austen's novels were particularly popular during the Second World War, possibly because 'the world they depicted contrasted so sharply with the horrific events of 1939–45' (p.ix). But, in fact, the prevalence of the game image in *Emma* draws our attention to how the idea of immutability and permanence is connected with a particular form of organisation and order. It may be that Austen, rather than *celebrating* the idea of a permanent society is subtly illuminating the way in which a society can deliberately foster a sense of its own permanence and stability by upholding a strict set of rules and hierarchical relations.

I now want to turn to the word-games in *Emma*. I think that they also function to illuminate something about Highbury society, but they have a rather different significance from the other games in the book. The two particular examples of word-games that I want to look at are the collection of riddles and conundrums of chapter 9, and the alphabet game of chapter 41. Of all the games in the book, Austen describes these in the most detail. Indeed, they play an important part in advancing the plot. In chapter 9, Austen describes how Emma and Harriet collect together a number of riddles, enigmas and conundrums. Mr Elton takes this opportunity to give Emma a charade which contains a hint of his intentions towards her. Emma swiftly solves the puzzle, finds the answer to be 'courtship', but mistakenly applies it to Harriet instead of herself. Similarly, in chapter 41, while the others are innocently engaged in making anagrams out of the letters of the alphabet, Frank Churchill exploits the situation to send pointed messages to Jane Fairfax. Mr Knightley, observing this, thinks indignantly, 'It was a child's play, chosen to conceal a deeper game on Frank Churchill's part' (chapter 41).

The alphabet game in fact provides Austen with an ideal

opportunity to dramatise the various perspectives and understandings of the major characters in the book. Frank Churchill and Jane Fairfax are, literally and figuratively, playing a 'secret game', hidden from everybody else. Emma and Harriet, participants in both the alphabet game and the 'adult game' of matchmaking, cannot see what is going on. Only Mr Knightley, a detached observer both of this game and, as he thinks at this stage, of the courtship game, can see, to some extent, what is going on.

But if we focus more directly on the word-games themselves, what is important about them is that they are about language and communication. The riddle and conundrum games involve making sense out of nonsensical rhymes. The alphabet game is about turning jumbles of letters into recognisable words. The rules and discipline of these games are directed towards ordering language and making it into messages that communicate a sense to someone else. Thus, Emma forms the message 'courtship' out of Mr Elton's charade and Jane Fairfax makes the words 'blunder' and 'Dixon' from Frank's jumbled letters. Moreover, these games are not just about *ordering* language into meaningful messages, they are also about *interpreting* those messages. Emma has to decide what 'courtship' means and concludes that it is a message to Harriet from a would-be lover. Jane has to interpret the significance of Frank's cryptic hints, 'blunder' and 'Dixon', and realises that she is being taunted by her piqued lover.

However, the activity of interpretation is a complicated one and depends largely on what ideas and understanding each person brings to it. Because of this, there is always the possibility of a variety of different interpretations being made. Thus, because Emma brings her own matchmaking plans to her interpretation of Mr Elton's charade, she interprets it as a message to Harriet. Later, in the alphabet game, she interprets the word 'Dixon' as a reference to her guess that Jane is secretly in love with her friend's husband. Jane, on the other hand, is able to interpret it correctly as a shared joke between herself and Frank at Emma's expense.

I suggest that, as Austen uses board- and card-games to represent the way in which Highbury society organises itself, so she uses these word-games to symbolise the way in which communication between its members is carried on. Throughout *Emma*, the members of the Highbury circle have to interpret each other's words and actions. All too often, the interpretations differ as misunderstandings arise. Mr Elton and Emma's mutual misinterpretation of each other's words and behaviour is a case in point. Perhaps even more disturbing is Emma's and Harriet's misinterpretation of each other. Emma, caught up in her own matchmaking schemes, takes Harriet's admission of regard for someone of high rank to be referring to Frank Churchill. Equally, Harriet takes Emma's assurance that 'there have been matches of greater disparity' as encouragement to think of Mr Knightley. On a later occasion, their mutual misinterpretations become clear. Emma has interpreted Harriet's profession of gratitude for a service rendered as referring to Frank rescuing her from the gipsies. Harriet replies, 'Oh, dear . . . now I recollect what you mean; but I was thinking of something very different at the time' (chapter 47).

It seems, then, that the activities of interpretation and making sense that go on in word-games represent the way that communication itself is carried on in society. What Austen underlines through her use of word-games is that there is no such thing as pure and simple communication. Rather, she shows, all communication is conducted by means of active efforts to make sense of and interpret another's words and actions. Because of this, when characters in *Emma* want to communicate something very important, they tend to fall silent, as though they feel that the less they say, the more chance the other person will have of interpreting them correctly. Thus, Mr Knightley says, when declaring has feelings for Emma: 'I cannot make speeches, Emma . . . If I loved you less, I might be able to talk about it more.' (chapter 49).

I would like to conclude by suggesting that Austen does not restrict what she says about communication to spoken words. The word-games involve written words and letters. Writing also needs to be interpreted, including, of course, the writing of the book *Emma* itself. Intriguingly, the answer to one of the word-games in the book is 'Emma'. On Box Hill, Mr Weston produces the conundrum, 'What two letters of the alphabet are there, that express perfection?' (chapter 43). The answer is 'M and A. — Emma'. This is, of course, not only the name of the main character, but also the title of the book itself. Could Austen be hinting that we need to approach her book like a word-game? That we need to be prepared to read it *actively*, to interpret its meaning according to the ways of understanding we bring to it?

It is only by this kind of active engagement with the text that I have been able to answer my own question about the significance of games in *Emma*. Austen does not make it explicit that she intends them to be read symbolically or used to comment on aspects of Highbury's social organisation and ways of communication. However, games of all kinds do feature prominently throughout the novel, suggesting that they have a greater significance than as mere details of Highbury domestic life. I have tried to show in this essay that if the characteristics of these games are examined closely, they illuminate and criticise the organisation, order and communication of Highbury society, and indeed of the novel *Emma* itself.

AFTERTHOUGHTS

1

What analogies are drawn in this essay between games and social organisation?

2

Do you agree that the inhabitants of Highbury 'ignore the existence of any world outside its confines' (page 40)?

3

What special significance does Campbell see in word-games?

4

What do you understand by 'active engagement with the text' (last paragraph)?

Mark Spencer-Ellis

*Mark Spencer-Ellis is Head of English
at Forest School, and an experienced
A-level examiner. He has edited* Brave
New World *and* Cry the Beloved
Country *for Longman Study Texts.*

ESSAY

Definition and self-definition

The words *seem/seems/seemed* occur over seventy times in
Emma; there are almost as many instances of *real/really/in
reality*. We make sense of these terms by seeing them as opposites, and by correctly identifying them we arrive at the truth.
True/truth/truly also occur on nearly fifty occasions. The vocabulary provides a structure which leads to a reassuring experience for the reader. We unravel the real motives of characters
and their true feelings. Sometimes our understanding is in
advance of theirs; sometimes we play the detective about events.
And eventually we all happily arrive at the end of the book,
having solved the mysteries and comprehended the characters.
The completeness of our response is directed by the way in
which everyone is finally partnered by the most convenient
mate, and 'happily-ever-after' is all that seems to be missing.

However, once you start to examine the terms used to
express approval or disapproval, such a response to the novel
becomes far less satisfying. For example in chapter 12 when the
greetings between the Knightley brothers 'succeeded in the true
English style', what do we understand by 'true'? The rest of the
sentence provides a gloss: this style consists of 'burying under
a calmness that seemed all but indifference, the real attachment

46

which would have led either of them, if requisite, to do every thing for the good of the other'. So 'true' suggests something a bit deceptive, or at least not overt and demonstrative, and allied to a 'real' attachment. But 'real' is pretty open-ended as well. Where would either Mr Knightley draw the line in assisting his brother? Law-breaking? Lying? We don't know for sure. Nor, more importantly, can we tell how to define 'the good of the other'. Is this to be understood in material or in moral terms? *Emma* is written in the vocabulary of certainty — a language which suggests that we can arrive at perceptions which are undeniably 'true' — but trying to pin down the reference points for the judgements may serve to undermine the certainties.

'Handsome, clever, and rich' seems a straightforward enough description of Emma herself. But you won't appreciate the force of the words by looking them up individually in a dictionary. Their impact depends upon their being grouped; in the context of the novel's opening paragraph the words form a single unit, each depending on the other. Can one be handsome and clever without being rich? A little thought about Jane Fairfax's possible fate as a governess suggests that she would quickly forfeit any claim to the first two titles had she gone to Mrs Smallridge's. Beauty and brains need money. One cannot possibly imagine Miss Bates as handsome and clever, even when Emma's age, nor would Jane Fairfax's qualities outlast the financial support of Colonel Campbell.

A convincing case can be made for cash being the central reference point for these terms of judgement. There is no need to rehearse all the financial considerations which go into marriage, nor the extent to which Emma herself is defined as a commodity. When she reflects angrily on the motives for Mr Elton's proposal to her and his discovery that 'Miss Woodhouse of Hartfield, the heiress of thirty thousand pounds, [was] not quite so easily obtained as he had fancied' (chapter 16), she doesn't dispute the values, simply Mr Elton's assumption that he is a prospective purchaser. 'Of Hartfield' isn't simply an address either. The house reflects the way in which its inhabitants like to see themselves as existing in total independence from the rest of society. But this 'independence' is illusory, for the author carefully places the house within: 'Highbury, the large and populous village almost amounting to a town, to which

Hartfield, in spite of its separate lawn and shrubberies and name, did really belong' (chapter 1). The characters like to see themselves as subject only to their own emotions and reason, but what they are worth is what determines how others value them. John Knightley cuts through Jane Fairfax's polite speculation about what lies behind the efficiency of post-office clerks: '"If you want any further explanation," continued he, smiling, "they are paid for it. That is the key to a great deal of capacity."' (chapter 34).

Emma's own education throughout the novel, her growing social awareness and knowledge of her own emotions, suggests that it is possible to arrive at a clearly identifiable truth about all issues. Her contempt for Robert Martin isn't simply snobbery; it suggests a wilful shutting out of facts she doesn't want to recognise. 'He will be a completely gross, vulgar farmer — totally inattentive to appearances, and thinking of nothing but profit and loss,' she remarks to Harriet (chapter 4). Notice how the terms of disapproval seem to merge. Are all farmers necessarily gross and vulgar? Are profit and loss shameful in themselves, or is the fault in thinking about them? The sentence suggests that all these qualities are axiomatically linked, but they disentangle themselves when analysed separately. Emma herself quickly finds that farming topics, the new bailiff who must have been hired to improve profits, are what she has to resort to if John Knightley is to be prevented from saying something upsetting to her father: '"I did not thoroughly understand what you were telling your brother," cried Emma, "about your friend Mr Graham's intending to have a bailiff from Scotland, to look after his new estate."' (chapter 12). Mr Knightley, in the same chapter, shifts his brother's attention to practical farming matters: 'But, John, as to what I was telling you of my idea of moving the path to Langham, of turning it more to the right that it may not cut through the home meadows, I cannot conceive any difficulty'. Is this gross or vulgar?

A similar shift is shown in the way in which the law is perceived. Running through possible suitors for Harriet, Emma briskly dismisses the thought of William Cox: 'Oh! no, I could not endure William Cox — a pert young lawyer' (chapter 16). Does Emma's imagination stretch to there being gentlemanly young lawyers or do her words express a complete judgement on all young members of the profession? Mrs Elton's social status is clinically analysed in chapter 22: 'an uncle remained — in the law line — nothing more distinctly honourable was hazarded of him, than that he was in the law line'. Lawyers are the acceptable face of trade — the world of profit and loss which is the base of Emma's society but which her values prefer to ignore: 'The landed property of Hartfield certainly was inconsiderable, being but a sort of notch in the Donwell Abbey estate, to which all the rest of Highbury belonged; but their fortune, from other sources, was such as to make them scarcely secondary to Donwell Abbey itself, in every other kind of consequence' (chapter 16). What 'other sources'? Hesitancy and distaste accompany the very word applicable to Mrs Elton's father: 'Miss Hawkins was the youngest of the two daughters of a Bristol — merchant, of course, he must be called' (chapter 22). Yet the man Emma marries is a farmer, and his brother a lawyer.

However, if we go along with Emma and end up with the tacit acknowledgement that farmers and lawyers can be acceptable, that William Larkins isn't a pleasant rustic comic but the holder of a vital office in the Donwell estate, and even that trade is what provides her standard of living, we are still reading the book as a quest for right answers, for the truth. But there are problems if we see the symmetrical ending as a final understanding of character and action.

To begin with, there is the old question of what sort of a married life awaits Emma and Mr Knightley. It isn't easy to imagine much in the way of development: children probably, but what else? Amusingly and innocently, emotional and sexual experience is pointed by references to the sea. Emma herself seems strangely intense in her response to the topic: 'I must beg you not to talk of the sea. It makes me envious and miserable; — I who have never seen it!' (chapter 12). Mr Woodhouse, unsurprisingly, finds the whole idea far too much for him. He is convinced that 'the sea is very rarely of use to anybody', and even states: 'I am sure it almost killed me once'. That resolute family man Mr John Knightley takes his wife and children to South End for the autumn but his father-in-law supports the claims of Cromer on the grounds that the real danger can be kept at a safe distance: 'And, by what I understand, you might have had lodgings there quite away from the sea — a quarter

of a mile off — very comfortable' (ibid.). And Emma's speculation about a possible attachment between Jane Fairfax and Mr
Dixon is heightened by the incident when: 'she, by the sudden
whirling round of something or other among the sails, would
have been dashed into the sea at once, and actually was all but
gone, if he had not, with the greatest presence of mind, caught
hold of her habit' (chapter 19). Perhaps Mr Knightley will take
his new wife to the seaside, but then what?

While the Emma — Mr Knightley relationship may be the
most obvious unanswered problem at the end of the novel, it
is not the only aspect of our final response in which apparent
'solutions' simply raise more questions. The very neatness of the
final line-up is just a bit too reassuring for the reader: Harriet
and Robert Martin, linked in class in spite of Emma's earlier
plans; the openly ambitious Mr and Mrs Elton; the novel's two
enigmas, Jane Fairfax and Frank Churchill; and finally Emma
herself and Mr Knightley. But for the three couples for whom
the book tries to engage our emotional sympathies, the arti-
ficialities of the plot which engineer their second chances serve
only to make us aware that in 'real life' you make a mess of a
relationship and usually have to live with the consequences.
Most Harriets wouldn't get a second proposal from Robert
Martin. The novel neatly avoids facing up to this by giving us
an image of the man expressed entirely through the values of
other characters, especially Mr Knightley. The open-ended
reference, 'Robert Martin's manners have sense, sincerity, and
good-humour to recommend them; and his mind has more true
gentility than Harriet Smith could understand' (chapter 8),
produces a do-it-yourself effect: we can even leave the reference
points vague, and consequently we don't invent a Robert Martin
who shrugs his shoulders on being turned down, and quickly
finds a girl a notch or two further up the ladder of 'true
gentility'.

The two events which lead to the happy ending are conspicuously unrelated to anything realistically arising from the novel.
The death of Mrs Churchill is conveniently produced just late
enough to ensure that we realise that the logical progression
of their situation is not a happy marriage for Jane Fairfax
and Frank Churchill but, for her, the misery of governess-trade,
memorably compared by her to the slave-trade: 'widely different

certainly as to the guilt of those who carry it on; but as to the greater misery of the victims, I do not know where it lies' (chapter 35). For Frank, no doubt, the logical progression of their situation is a period of grief and regret abroad, followed by a suitable courtship and marriage back in England. Our imagination finds it difficult to see Emma and Mr Knightley progressing beyond their engagement partly because of the circumstance which does allow the marriage to take place. The absurdity of the turkey theft — the Westons' poultry-yard making its only appearance in the final chapter so as to bring forward the wedding — prods us into realising that the whole ending is so contrived that the only thoughtful response must be to see that it simply draws attention to its not being a satisfactory solution to the story. You can't ask a reader to assess characters as if they are real human beings, and then lean out of the sky to organise their lives to fit into the happily-ever-after ending.

While the ending signally fails to solve problems simply by providing a symmetrical plot, so the whole world of certain values, firmly implied in the vocabulary, fails in the end to suggest anything clearly defined as 'real' or 'true'. We can see how Emma is brought to adjust her judgements but our final response is more than an adjustment to our assessment of the social standing of farmers or of lawyers. A useful yardstick is our responses to Mrs Elton. If we take it for granted that readers follow the text's directions and disapprove of her, what are the precise grounds on which disapproval is based?

In fact it is very difficult to find grounds of condemnation which go beyond presumption. Mrs Elton understands the rules; the problem — from Emma's point of view — is that she sees herself as a social referee rather than as someone who should know her place, a place several rungs below Emma. Mrs Elton is given one of the better snobbish lines in the book: 'One has not great hopes from Birmingham'. Put that into a literary quiz and plenty of contestants will suggest Oscar Wilde as the author. But in context (chapter 36) it illustrates a complicated situation where the social climber from the laughably vulgar Bristol is exposing herself by looking down on the source of unmentionable manufacturing wealth, Birmingham. Mrs Elton is a parody of Emma. She takes it upon herself to organise Jane

Fairfax's life just as Emma does for Harriet. What upsets Emma is emphatically not Mrs Elton's professed standards of judgement — that Mrs Weston 'is really quite the gentlewoman' (chapter 32) or even 'that Mr Knightley is a gentleman' (ibid.) — but her presumption in deciding that she is in a position to pass these judgements. If we disapprove of Mrs Elton for assuming precedence over Emma at the ball and in the expedition to Box Hill we are still accepting the social code which arranges people in such strict order. Mrs Elton's function is to expose the social values which are usually politely concealed.

Mrs Elton's vocabulary in chapter 32 when we first meet her reveals this function: 'I really could not help exclaiming'; 'there is nothing like staying at home for real comfort'; 'I really cannot get this girl to move from the house'; 'I really could not give it a thought'; 'but really when I looked about my acquaintance, I tremble'; 'but really I begin now to comprehend that a married woman has many things to call to her attention'; 'she is really quite the gentlewoman'. We read her use of 'really' as a signal that she's trying too hard. What is being stressed is not that Mrs Weston is being some kind of a phoney gentlewoman, but that Mrs Elton is claiming the right to make these statements. And the more Mrs Elton says 'really' the more we register the insincerity of the remark.

If that is the case, how are we to read the following remarks, also taken from direct speech: 'you have been repeatedly in the company of some, such very real gentlemen' (chapter 4); 'I cannot really change for the better' (chapter 10); 'I really think you may say what you like of your acquaintance with her' (chapter 24); 'the superior companions who have always loved her with such real, generous affection' (chapter 33); or 'you know we are not really so much brother and sister as to make it at all improper' (chapter 38)? Of course, all these remarks are made by Emma, and our understanding of *real/really* depends on the extent to which we accept Emma's right to make judgements. On the whole we feel ourselves free to question Emma's judgements but not her sincerity. More important, when we disagree with her we aren't disputing the assumption that there are *real* gentlemen, that there can be *real* generous affection, or that relationships can be *really* defined.

However, if these terms prove so slippery when in direct speech, how are we to read them when they are produced with the authority of the writer? The authorial voice, at different moments in the novel, links the following words with *real*: good will, attachment, affection, love, opinion, feeling, anxiety, alarm, pleasure and misery. Are we to question the text's sincerity, to imagine Jane Austen telling us 'this is what I really did imagine', or does the overwhelming number of claims for a quality being the genuine article eventually serve to undermine the assumption that these terms of judgement can finally be tied down to precise reference points?

The encounter between Emma and Frank Churchill in chapter 24, and the subsequent speculation about him at the beginning of chapter 25, is marked by a great cluster of these words. In this scene Emma and the reader are prompted to make mistakes about both Frank Churchill and Jane Fairfax. There is, within a few pages, *appear/appeared* and *seem/seems* six times each, and five instances of *really*. The words which encourage us to assume that we can solve a situation serve to mislead us. The aim is 'to form a reasonable judgement', as Emma hopes to do on the subject of Frank, but when the plot is untangled we are not satisfied by such a contrived 'truth' as the one offered in the ending.

The reassuring word *blunder* suggests how the codes of behaviour are assumed to be stable. The implications of the word are that a mistake, a gross mistake, has been made but that it is not the sort of flagrant rule-breaking which would get you expelled from the game. A blunder might be to let in an easy goal but it wouldn't cover sawing down your goal-posts or setting fire to the ball. The framework of society with you still in it is not changed by a blunder. While the most obvious instance is the word-game in which Frank Churchill gives Jane Fairfax the letters of the word, it is revealing that eight of the twelve instances of *blunder/blundered* refer to Emma's mistakes. And it is equally revealing that the language of definition in *Emma* has to fall back on negatives to describe what lies, and is known to lie, beyond its particular social world. There are no words which can refer directly to Harriet's station if she is not part of the Highbury world: 'She is the natural daughter of nobody knows whom, with probably no settled provision at all, and certainly no respectable relations' (chapter 8).

When we read *Emma*, both the terms of definition and the plot turn back on themselves. The vocabulary and the structure suggest a world of knowable certainty, and a society peopled by individuals all with their own different emotions and motives. However, just as the idea of the self-contained individual becomes less and less convincing — both of the tyrants, Mr Woodhouse and Mrs Churchill, are essential parts of Emma and Frank Churchill — so we are left unclear about how we are to understand all these terms which suggest clear values. The language of certainty leaves us with a final impression of uncertainty, not a society well-defined and sure of itself but one built on shifting sands.

AFTERTHOUGHTS

Is it legitimate to speculate on 'what sort of a married life awaits Emma and Mr Knightley' (page 49)?

Do you agree with Spencer-Ellis's interpretation of references to the sea in *Emma* (pages 49–50)?

Explain Spencer-Ellis's argument that it is difficult to find reasons for our disapproval of Mrs Elton that 'go beyond presumption' (page 51). Do you agree?

What is the fundamental purpose behind Spencer-Ellis's close analysis in this essay of the way language is used in *Emma*?

Catherine Neale

Catherine Neale is Senior Lecturer in English at Worcester College of Higher Education, and author of the Penguin Masterstudy on Middlemarch.

ESSAY

Emma: the role of heroine and the role of woman

Emma, as the eponymous heroine, and as a character within the pages of that novel, claims the reader's immediate and full attention. From the opening sentence, she is the central focus of the narrative. In a first reading of the novel, there is considerable mystery, comic surprise, and eventual revelation: these effects are caused by the reader's apprehension of characters and events primarily through Emma's eyes. Subsequent readings develop the ironic distance between Emma and the narrating voice, yet we still follow Emma to the exclusion of many other, potentially interesting characters in the novel. She is, then, quite simply, the 'heroine' of the novel.

Jane Austen's habitual and at times perverse irony is evident in her famous description of Emma: 'I am going to take a heroine whom no one but myself will much like'.[1] While many readers debate how likeable Emma is as a *character*, fewer consider the degree to which Emma as a *heroine* is ac-

---

[1] J E Austen-Leigh, *A Memoir of Jane Austen*, reprinted in *Persuasion* (London, 1965), pp.375–376.

ceptable, or 'likeable'. Yet Jane Austen's irony is always fully directed at the notion of fictional stereotypes, and particularly at fictional heroines. Her writing displays an awareness of the gap between fiction and reality, and interrogates the assumed qualities of the 'heroine', her customary career in the course of the novel, and her final, inevitable qualification for marriage.

An avid reader, from the beginning of her writing career, Jane Austen consistently parodied, satirised and rewrote the fiction that she and her family enjoyed. In the novels of Samuel Richardson, she found a demonstration of the fruitful possibilities of the epistolary style, and these novels contain heroines such as Pamela, who rises through fortitude and resistance to marry her master, and Clarissa, whose liveliness and attractiveness lead to her rape and lingering death. In Gothic novels of the late eighteenth century (for example, *The Mysteries of Udolpho* by Anne Radcliffe, to which Jane Austen pays mocking tribute in *Northanger Abbey*), the conventional heroine is meek, good, feminine and threatened with all kinds of horrors, including, usually, a fatally attractive villain. With specific reference to *Emma*, a novel entitled *Discipline* by Mary Brunton, published in 1815, portrays a heroine who has been indulged from infancy, and, free from a mother's restraining influence, must conform and learn to deserve her high social position through a series of unfortunate experiences. In addition, one critic has demonstrated the influence of the tale of a high-spirited and romantically inclined girl in *The Heroine, or Adventures of Cherubina* (1813) by Eaton Stannard Barrett, and has shown that the sentimental stereotype of a dutiful daughter in a play, *The Birthday* (1799) by Kotzebue, is reworked in *Emma*.[2]

In a humorous 'Plan' of a novel, probably dating from 1816, Jane Austen underlines the difference between fictional type and character by her short-hand references to the heroine; the stereotype described in her perfection swamps any notion of characterisation:

---

[2] Margaret Kirkham, *Jane Austen, Feminism and Fiction* (Sussex, 1983), pp.121–143.

Scene to be in the Country, Heroine the Daughter of a Clergyman ... Heroine a faultless Character herself — , perfectly good, with much tenderness & sentiment, & not the least Wit — very highly accomplished, understanding modern Languages & (generally speaking) everything that the most accomplished young Women learn, but particularly excelling in Music — her favourite pursuit — & playing equally well on the Piano Forte & Harp — & singing in the first stile. Her Person, quite beautiful — dark eyes & plump cheeks.

(*Minor Works*, ed. R W Chapman

(London, 1969), p.428)

This 'Plan' was a mocking response to the Prince Regent's Librarian, who had ventured to suggest a subject for Jane Austen's novelistic attention. The conventional and even dreary attributes of the 'heroine' are here skilfully sketched in: 'perfect' goodness, intelligence, musicianship and beauty. In early work, too, Jane Austen played with the nonsensical extravagances of other writers describing heroines. For example, in 'Love and Freindship' (*sic*), a juvenile piece dating from 1790, Laura writes to Marianne:

My Father was a native of Ireland & an inhabitant of Wales; My Mother was the natural Daughter of a Scotch Peer by an italian Opera-girl — I was born in Spain & received my Education at a Convent in France.

When I had reached my eighteenth Year I was recalled by my Parents to my paternal roof in Wales. Our mansion was situated in one of the most romantic parts of the Vale of Uske. Tho' my Charms are now considerably softened and somewhat impaired by the Misfortunes I have undergone, I was once beautiful. But lovely as I was the Graces of my Person were the least of my Perfections. Of every accomplishment accustomary to my sex, I was Mistress. When in the Convent, my progress had always exceeded my instructions, my Acquirements had been wonderfull for my Ages, and I had shortly surpassed my Masters.

In my Mind, every Virtue that could adorn it was centered; it was the Rendezvous of every good Quality & of every noble sentiment.

(ibid., pp.77–78)

Reading beyond the parody and comedy, we may discern the habitual traits of this kind of literary heroine: she has an exotic background, high social status ('our mansion'), a romantic disposition, and, of course, beauty, intelligence and virtue. They may be summed up in the word 'perfection'.

In the Juvenilia, Jane Austen frequently used the first-person narrative to create dramatic irony and bathos. This remains in the letters that appear within the novels; generally, however, the published fiction disavows that narrative viewpoint and instead a powerful authorial voice distances the characters. The result is that they are held up for examination, both as characters and as fictional types. In the novels which do not carry two parallel heroines (for example, *Sense and Sensibility*, in which two sisters, Elinor and Marianne, are contrasted ironically in their differing attitudes and temperaments) other features of the 'heroine' are shown: each solitary heroine is a rewriting of the conventional heroine. In *Northanger Abbey*, we are told at the beginning:

> No one who had ever seen Catherine Morland in her infancy, would have supposed her born to be an heroine. Her situation in life, the character of her father and mother, her own person and disposition, were all equally against her.
>
> (chapter 1)

Catherine is, as we find out, ordinary, happy, plain and matter-of-fact. In *Mansfield Park*, the heroine Fanny Price is a poor relation, and is quiet, timid, and pretty rather than beautiful. In *Persuasion*, Anne Elliot is twenty-seven years old, and has suffered a disappointment in love:

> A few years before, Anne Elliot had been a very pretty girl, but her bloom had vanished early; and as, even in its height, her father had found little to admire in her (so totally different were her delicate features and mild dark eyes from his own); there could be nothing in them, now that she was faded and thin, to excite his esteem.
>
> (chapter 1)

Anne's faded looks and her age act as a challenge to received ideas of the ideal heroine. The 'heroine', of course, is to marry; that is, in general, to be her story. Many of the ideal heroine's qualities are part of what sociologists call 'the social construction of femininity': qualities which are perceived as being appropriately feminine, such as refinement, skill in activities like music and painting, quietness or submissiveness, and beauty. They must be inculcated and learned, turning what is female into what is feminine, and in much of western culture, including the novels of Jane Austen, femininity is what makes a woman desirable and marriageable. Catherine Morland, Fanny Price and Anne Elliott are, as has been seen, deliberately unconventional heroines, but their stories all end with marriage: Jane Austen, in doing this, 'rewrites' the heroine but retains her story.

Emma Woodhouse is perhaps the most ambitious rewriting of the heroine — a fact signalled in Jane Austen's statement of intention — precisely because she appears to possess all those conventional qualities:

> Emma Woodhouse, handsome, clever, and rich, with a comfortable home and happy disposition, seemed to unite some of the best blessings of existence; and had lived nearly twenty-one years in the world with very little to distress or vex her.

She is obedient to her father, gracious and intelligent. But, as heroine, she awkwardly has neither desire nor reason to marry. She tells Harriet:

> I have none of the usual inducements of women to marry. Were I to fall in love, indeed, it would be a different thing! but I never have been in love; it is not my way, or my nature; and I do not think I ever shall. And, without love, I am sure I should be a fool to change such a situation as mine. Fortune I do not want; employment I do not want; consequence I do not want: I believe few married women are half as much mistress of their husband's house, as I am of Hartfield; and never, never could I expect to be so truly beloved and important; so always first and always right in any man's eyes as I am in my father's.

(chapter 10)

Emma's observations shrewdly identify that the underlying reason for women to marry is financial, within a society where women have little legal status or scope for independent employment. Emma is produced by Jane Austen as the ideal heroine, but in her situation of feeling no need nor desire for marriage, she exposes assumptions about the role of women that lurk within the fictional production of the heroine.

There are four other significant female characters in *Emma*, who serve to highlight the heroine and her situation. The novel begins with Miss Taylor's marriage to Mr Weston, an event which Mr Knightley places in its pragmatic context:

> Poor Mr and Miss Woodhouse, if you please; but I cannot possibly say 'poor Miss Taylor.' I have a great regard for you and Emma; but when it comes to the question of dependence or independence! . . . [Emma] knows how much the marriage is to Miss Taylor's advantage; she knows how very acceptable it must be at Miss Taylor's time of life to be settled in a home of her own, and how important to her to be secure of a comfortable provision . . .
>
> (chapter 1)

Miss Taylor has no financial security in remaining a governess to a charge who has already grown up. Her marriage is, in fact, a great blessing and security for her. This is somewhat confirmed in the situation of Miss Bates, much older than Miss Taylor and ensconced in a comfortable spinsterly role, but subject to poverty and to the tribulations of remaining unmarried in this society. Once again, it is Mr Knightley who observes the realities of her situation: 'She is poor; she has sunk from the comforts she was born to; and, if she live to old age, must probably sink more. Her situation should secure your compassion.' (chapter 43).

Jane Fairfax's role in the novel is more complex than those of Miss Taylor or Miss Bates. She is elegant, refined and intelligent, noted for her musicianship, and has been educated to become a governess, 'the very few hundred pounds which she inherited from her father making independence impossible' (chapter 20). Emma's discomfort with her derives from an awareness of the superiority of her attainments and an uncomfortable sense that there is little to distinguish between them otherwise except that Emma does have financial security. While Emma can afford to reject the prospect of marriage, for Jane Fairfax marriage would save her from the career of governess that she regards with horror. Emma turns for companionship to

Harriet Smith, the pretty young girl who, as Mr Knightley discerns yet again, 'is a girl who will marry somebody or other' (chapter 8); despite her lack of money and background, Harriet is quintessentially feminine and will therefore always find someone to marry. Emma can therefore condescend to regard marriage as appropriate for someone like Harriet, in whom she need not contemplate the less pleasant alternatives for women.

In Emma Woodhouse, then, the novel *Emma* holds up for the reader a potentially radical and disturbing heroine, who does not wish nor need to marry. But Jane Austen was no feminist writer in this sense. The novel creates a problem but copes with it by giving Emma certain traits which need to be 'improved'. She is flawed by her snobbishness, her wilfulness, her meddling in the affairs of other people, and finally her rudeness to Miss Bates. The novel shows how she is educated through her mistakes and by repeated conversations with Mr Knightley. There is nothing morally flawed in her: the prevailing effect of her actions is always comic rather than tragic. She reaches understanding of herself and is rewarded with Mr Knightley's love. This process of change and development in Emma is the ideological drift of the novel. However, it is possible to read 'against the grain', and to read quite a different story in this heroine's experiences.

In Miss Taylor and Jane Fairfax, we see the anxieties and pain of the single woman as governess hinted at. There is also, in Miss Taylor in particular, a study of the educative role of governess. Female education, in this novel and in this section of society at the time at which Jane Austen was writing, is and was aimed at producing femininity, and is and was often achieved through a governess, her role being to prepare her charges for marriage through the acquisition of feminine skills. Jane Austen was interested in the governess figure from the beginning of her writing career. In 'Jack and Alice', dating from between 1787 and 1790, a situation very similar to Emma's at the beginning of *Emma* is described, but with a vital difference. This heroine was six when her mother died, and as her brothers were sent away to school and her sisters were still in the nursery, her father left her alone in the care of a governess:

Miss Dickins was an excellent Governess. She instructed me in the Paths of Virtue; under her tuition I daily became more amiable, & might perhaps by this time have nearly attained perfection, had not my worthy Preceptoress been torn from my arms, e'er I had attained my seventeenth year. I never shall forget her last words. "My dear Kitty she said, Good night t'ye." I never saw her afterwards,' continued Lady Williams wiping her eyes, 'She eloped with the Butler the same night.

> (*Minor Works*, ed. R W Chapman (London, 1969), p.17)

Evidently, by the time that Jane Austen came to write *Emma*, she was less interested in such broad bathetic effects than in the underlying themes of education and of the influence of teachers such as the governess. Miss Taylor has been torn from Emma just as rudely, in Mr Woodhouse's view:

> Poor Miss Taylor! — I wish she were here again. What a pity it is that Mr Weston ever thought of her! . . . it will be a great comfort to poor Miss Taylor to have somebody about her that she is used to see.
>
> (chapter 1)

She has, of course, also left Emma in a far more respectable manner, in marrying Mr Weston. But the effects may well be similar: in Lady Williams's confession that she 'might by this time have nearly attained perfection', had not her governess disappeared, we meet again the requirement for some kind of 'perfection' in the heroine, which is debated in *Emma*.

From the beginning of the novel, Mr Knightley is 'one of the few people who could see faults in Emma Woodhouse, and the only one who ever told her of them' (chapter 1). Throughout the novel, there are discussions between Emma and Mr Knightley, during which he educates her. He tells Mrs Weston that Emma's education with her governess failed, because she did not learn feminine submissiveness:

> . . . ever since she was twelve, Emma has been mistress of the house and of you all. In her mother she lost the only person able to cope with her. She inherits her mother's talents, and must have been under subjection to her. . . . You are better placed *here*; very fit for a wife, but not at all for a governess. But you were preparing yourself to be an excellent wife all the time you

were at Hartfield. You might not give Emma such a complete education as your powers would seem to promise; but you were receiving a very good education from *her*, on the very material matrimonial point of submitting your own will, and doing as you were bid . . .

(chapter 5)

Emma's failure at this point is ostensibly that she has never applied herself to disciplined study; Mr Knightley's words here betray the real charge, that she has not learned to be feminine. She is, therefore, not 'perfect': immediately after her offensiveness to Miss Bates, she is given the conundrum by Mr Weston, 'What two letters of the alphabet are there, that express perfection? . . . M. and A. — Em — ma. Do you understand', to which Mr Knightley replies, '*Perfection* should not have come quite so soon.' (chapter 43).

The novel examines the ways in which this 'perfection' is gender-based. Emma thinks that she *is* perfect, despite her consciousness that Mr Knightley thinks otherwise. In his explanation to Mrs Weston, Mr Knightley comes close to suggesting that only mothers and men will succeed as educators, as they will understand the underlying objectives of female education: to construct femininity. It is Emma who has been an excellent governess to Miss Taylor, forcing her to be submissive and therefore preparing her to be Mrs Weston. Emma, as governess, bullies in the same way as Mr Knightley bullies *her*. Sensitive to the positions of Miss Taylor, Miss Bates and Jane Fairfax, as we have seen, Mr Knightley is therefore sensitive to the position of women in the society around him, and tries to make Emma see how women have to cope. By stressing the difficulties he moulds Emma into someone who wants to be a wife. She learns femininity and 'perfection' from him, and his proposal of marriage tellingly hinges on his educative role towards her:

> I have blamed you, and lectured you, and you have borne it as no other woman in England would have borne it. — Bear with the truths I would tell you now, dearest Emma, as well as you have borne with them. The manner, perhaps, may have as little to recommend them. God knows, I have been a very indifferent lover.

(chapter 49)

He has taught her to want to be married. And Emma, in her attitude towards first Miss Taylor and then Harriet, is engaged in the same exercise, although on more willing subjects. She trains Harriet in feminine refinement, not least in developing in Harriet an avid interest in matrimonial prospects, and ultimately she is successful here too. Harriet marries Robert Martin at the end of the novel, having become an improved and acceptable young lady. Mr Knightley congratulates Emma:

> I am convinced of her being an artless, amiable girl, with very good notions, very seriously good principles, and placing her happiness in the affections and utility of domestic life. — Much of this, I have no doubt, she may thank you for.
>
> (chapter 54)

This is a case of one educator congratulating another.

Emma's relationship with Harriet, and her incessant matchmaking, are often viewed as indications of a repressed fascination with marriage, a fascination to which she succumbs, as to her destiny.[3] However, it seems just as reasonable to suggest that her early rejection of marriage is a decision reached with some justification. Although in the ideology of the novel Emma has to discover romantic love and sexual desire, without which she is incomplete, from a different viewpoint we may observe that her relationship with her father protects her from marriage. She is supplied with his constant and uncritical affection, and she witnesses in him the absence of a need for married companionship, indeed, a veritable dislike of the disruptive effects of marriage. She is in a detached position as 'governess' and 'match-maker', the two terms being here synonymous: she is, therefore, the successful unmarried woman who need not worry about financial considerations.

Those faults of Emma — snobbishness, wilfulness, meddlesomeness, and rudeness — are faults primarily in the context of an ideal femininity. It is just as useful to note that what she has to lose in the course of the novel are qualities which she shares with Mr Knightley: strength of will, impatience with trivia and pettiness, honesty, independence of mind, and an

---

[3] See, for example, Tony Tanner, *Jane Austen* (London, 1986), pp178–182.

appreciation of class differences and sexual politics. While she may be said to use Harriet as her substitute in 'courtships' with Mr Elton, Frank Churchill and Mr Knightley, thus identifying herself with Harriet's brand of femininity, she is also intrigued about what makes men desire to marry. The reason why women marry is obvious to Emma, but men's reasons are less easy to discover. Harriet is the archetypal submissive and pretty woman, and even though Mr Knightley tells Emma that 'Men of sense ... do not want silly wives' (chapter 8), Emma is capable of seeing that some do. Her encounters with Mr Elton and Frank Churchill do not contradict her suspicion altogether: while Mr Elton is obviously attracted towards ladies with money, another feature of the Mrs Elton who appears in Highbury eventually is that she exhibits in her conversation a parody of submissiveness and femininity. And Frank Churchill's choice of Jane Fairfax is based on her elegance and good looks rather than on her sense: 'She is a complete angel. Look at her. Is she not an angel in every gesture? Observe the turn of her throat.' (chapter 54). Despite Mr Knightley's warning, then, Emma remains convinced of men's priorities, even being willing to believe that Mr Knightley is drawn into love with Harriet. Mr Knightley eventually chooses Emma as a result of his long process of educating *her* into being what Harriet, Jane Fairfax, and even Mrs Elton to some degree, represent, and that she has resisted. An additional twist, noted by many readers, is that in Emma's rejection for herself of Mr Elton and Frank Churchill, the adage is reversed to become 'Women of sense do not want silly husbands'.

All too often readers concur with Jane Austen and Mr Knightley that Emma needs to be brought down a peg or two, that she has failings that need to be corrected, that she should develop sympathy with other women, that the ending is a happy one. It is just as possible that in Emma we see a picture of the implications of the role of women in Jane Austen's society. They are forced for material reasons to see marriage as their only way of life, forced to be feminine and submissive in order to be marriageable, and punished — or educated, perhaps, in Emma's case — if they remain single. The truly radical question lurking in *Emma*, perhaps unwittingly, is, what might happen if women did *not* need to marry? What, therefore, would become of fiction's heroines, whose reason for being is that they shall marry? It takes Mr Knightley a long time to persuade Emma that she wishes to marry. In the end, social circumstances and the prospect of loneliness play as much a part in her desire for Mr Knightley as sexual longing does:

> The child to be born at Randalls must be a tie there even dearer than herself; and Mrs Weston's heart and time would be occupied by it. They should lose her; and, probably, in great measure, her husband also. — Frank Churchill would return among them no more; and Miss Fairfax, it was reasonable to suppose, would soon cease to belong to Highbury. They would be married, and settled either at or near Enscombe. All that were good would be withdrawn; and if to these losses, the loss of Donwell were to be added, what would remain of cheerful or of rational society within their reach?
>
> (chapter 48)

Ultimately, there is no sphere for Emma the independent single woman, and no space for Emma the single heroine. The 'unlike-able' heroine must marry the man who has moulded her into femininity and made her want to marry: that best of governesses, Mr Knightley.

AFTERTHOUGHTS

1

What distinctions does Neale draw between Emma as character and Emma as heroine?

2

What do you understand by 'the social construction of femininity' (page 60)?

3

What do you understand by reading 'against the grain' (page 62)?

4

'The truly radical question lurking in *Emma* . . . is what might happen if women did *not* need to marry' (page 66). Do you agree?

Andrew Gibson

Andrew Gibson is Lecturer in English Literature at Royal Holloway and Bedford New College, University of London.

ESSAY

'Imaginism' and objectivity in *Emma*

Jane Austen actually coined a word for Emma. She called her an 'imaginist'. The Oxford English Dictionary rather baldly defines the term as meaning simply 'an imaginative person'. But Jane Austen effectively gives us her own definition when she specifically refers to Emma as 'an imaginist ... on fire with speculation and foresight' (chapter 39). Emma is continually misled by what Knightley refers to as her 'errors of imagination' (chapter 41). Her 'imaginism' consists in precisely that. She constantly tends to take her own imaginings for objective truth. This makes her sound rather like Don Quixote, and she has sometimes been called a 'female Quixote'. But the way her imagination works actually owes very little to books. Knightley makes it clear that she is incapable of 'steady reading' (chapter 5). In this respect, Emma is quite unlike Cervantes's knight-errant. That is partly what makes Jane Austen's novel so original. Emma is a female Quixote without the conventional pretext of books for her delusions. We can't blame second-rate literature for Emma's errors. Her mind is itself largely responsible for the mistakes it gets trapped in. *Emma*, then, is very much a novel about misunderstanding, and the individual's responsibility for his or her own forms of understanding. It raises questions about judgement and knowledge — the difficulty of judging correctly, of seeing the truth. It is possibly most subtle in the way it shows 'imaginism' as clouding sound sense and impeding objective judgement.

Emma's 'imaginism' repeatedly leads her into mistakes and misconceptions. Much of the novel is itself a fine tissue of mirages, of distortions of what Jane Austen tells us is the 'objective truth'. It is full of elaborate suppositions developed by Emma, conjectures unfortunately doomed to prove false. Emma makes her first mistakes with Harriet and Elton. She misreads Elton's affections and, in Jane Austen's terms, she also overestimates Harriet's attractions, and Harriet's worth. Jane Austen's analysis of the situation is quite clear, and so is her attitude to it. Emma sees herself as Harriet's patron, and sees her own patronage of Harriet as an act of disinterested benevolence. We're told that Harriet 'would be loved as one to whom' Emma 'could be useful' (chapter 4). But Jane Austen goes beneath Emma's professed disinterest and exposes her essentially self-interested motives.

Emma is adopting a protégé. Her imagination casts her as the catalyst who will transform the ugly duckling into a swan. Emma decides that she will 'notice' Harriet, 'improve' her, and 'inform her opinions and her manners' (chapter 3). Emma herself will play the role of mentor and improver. But Jane Austen presents that role as one which flatters Emma's vanity, and indulges her will to power. By patronising Harriet, Emma wins tribute. She wins it from Harriet herself, who sees Emma as her guide and wise adviser. She also extracts it from others, like Mrs Weston, who tend to see her as Harriet's selflessly beneficent protectress. At the same time, Emma gives herself a flattering sense of unlimited command over an ignorant and subservient girl. Harriet is someone who can be summoned 'at any time' and is thus 'a valuable addition' to Emma's 'privileges' (chapter 4). More importantly, Harriet is meek, and defers to Emma's views. So she allows Emma the illusion of intellectual power, of wisdom and knowledge. As Knightley says, though she isn't aware of it, Harriet is 'a flatterer in all her ways' (chapter 5). She 'looks upon Emma as knowing every thing' (chapter 5). Emma particularly savours Harriet's *reverence*. But she has little interest in Harriet's reverence for her social superiority.

Almost all of the characters in the novel are willing to grant her that. They are far less likely to credit her with genuine powers of judgement. But that's precisely what Harriet's reverence allows Emma's imagination to dwell on. It gives Emma the illusion of possessing sound judgement and real knowledge. It allows her to think she's right.

Throughout the novel, of course, Jane Austen turns her irony on the way Emma uses Harriet for her own ends. But the irony emerges more clearly as the novel begins to draw to a close, before Emma sees her errors whole. Harriet assumes, for instance, that Emma, in her wisdom, must have known about Frank Churchill and Jane Fairfax's relationship before the news got abroad. She also assumes that Emma must have known about her own feelings for Knightley. She is wrong on both counts. She, too, has mistaken the objective facts. Far from being astute, Emma the 'imaginist' has been grossly imperceptive. She is similarly imperceptive about Elton, of course. When he declares his 'unexampled passion' for her in the carriage, she reproaches him for being 'so sensible' of 'the very great inequality' between him and Harriet (chapter 15). Emma's protest here might seem idealistically indifferent to questions of rank. But in fact Emma rejects Elton for the same reason that he rejects Harriet. She objects to his 'having the arrogance to raise his eyes to her' and neglecting differences in social position (chapter 16). After all, the Eltons are 'nobody' (ibid.). So Elton insults Emma twice over. His declaration insults her pride in her social position. But he also looks 'down upon *her* friend' (ibid. — author's italics). He refuses Emma the 'grateful respect' she felt was due to her as Harriet's friend (ibid.). Elton admires her as a woman, and as a woman worth loving. But Emma's imagination and her vanity are too sophisticated and too demanding to be content with humdrum admiration of that order. The 'imaginist' in her wanted and expected to be admired as Harriet's mentor and guardian. In a sense, Emma wanted to be admired as Harriet's *creator*, as the woman of sound judgement who spotted and nurtured Harriet's finer qualities. Her self-flattering imagination has led her to anticipate a peculiarly subtle form of homage from Elton. But all she gets is the more usual and cruder form of homage. The objective fact is an ardent profession of love, and Emma is furious.

As we'll see in a moment, Emma's illusion that Frank is in love with her is consistent with all this. Once again, her imagination misleads her, and flatters her vanity in doing so. But Emma also misunderstands Jane Fairfax's behaviour, imagining a relationship between Jane and Dixon. This, by contrast, might seem somewhat irrelevant, here. But in fact the reverse is true. Emma's delusions about Jane actually provide a rather subtle variant on the same theme. Once again, imagination errs, and does so in a way that is indirectly and insidiously self-flattering. It's important to remember that Emma has been 'prone to take disgust towards a girl so idolized and so cried up' long before Jane actually arrives on the scene (chapter 24). Miss Bates talks a great deal of Jane, of course, and others are full of her praise.

But Emma resents Jane for different reasons as well. For she herself secretly recognises Jane's talents and her worth. As Knightley suggests, she dislikes Jane because she sees in her 'the really accomplished young woman which she wanted to be thought herself' (chapter 20). Seen in this light, the motives behind Emma's imaginary suspicions of Jane become much clearer. Her imagination allows her spuriously to exalt herself at Jane's expense. It grants her a position superior to Jane's, and not just in the obvious, social sense. Again, for Emma, that in itself would not be enough. When Emma first comes up with the 'ingenious and animating suspicion' that Jane has been involved with Dixon, her assumptions are not just false (chapter 19). They are extremely demeaning to Jane. Emma imagines Jane to be guilty of thoroughly 'mischievous' conduct (chapter 20). She imagines Jane, in fact, as 'having seduced Mr Dixon's affections from his wife' (ibid.). Emma's fantasy thus includes and serves as a basis for a fantasy of moral superiority to Jane.

Jane Austen clearly mocks such 'imaginism' as wild extravagance, and Emma herself quickly realises that these initial suspicions are obviously wrongheaded. But she doesn't do so because she discovers the objective truth. Jane Austen's irony is subtler than that. It was Miss Bates's stories which first encouraged Emma's imaginings, before Jane arrived in Highbury. But when Emma actually sees Jane, the image of Jane the temptress promptly dissolves. A Jane with a noticeable 'appearance of ill-health' will not sustain it (chapter 20). So Emma's attitude changes to one of pity. The pity grows more intense as she thinks of Jane's talent and elegance as going to waste in the future — as they are presumably likely to do, given Jane's luckless situation, her 'closing prospects' (chapter 45). More important still, Emma pities Jane the more as she dwells on the notion of her as ensnared in a hopeless love, 'a simple, single, successless love on her side alone, a 'sad poison' (chapter 20). Emma has no more evidence for this view of Jane's relationship with Dixon than she had for the first one. It's been produced partly by a romantically extreme imagination. Emma is eager to see Jane as suffering the melancholy pangs of unrequited love. Under the romanticism, however — and the touch of cruelty that accompanies it — Emma's new fantasy of Jane's plight is, once again, indirectly self-flattering. Emma is still demeaning Jane. But her initial conception of Jane as effectively immoral was *crudely* demeaning. It was in fact too crude to satisfy Emma's sophisticated imagination. So she substitutes a more subtly demeaning view of Jane as a terribly pitiable figure, deserving only 'compassion and respect' (ibid.). Either way, Emma derives a comforting sense of superiority from her own fantasy. As a respectable woman, she can reflect with 'complacency' on Jane's guilt (ibid.). If she has to discard the notion of Jane as temptress, then she can console herself with 'softened, charitable feelings', since Jane's 'beauty' is apparently 'destined to come to naught' (ibid.). Poor Jane is condemned to a dreary and unhappy future. That fact allows Emma to look down commiseratingly upon her. Emma can even think with pleasure of her own comfort and ease, as opposed to Jane's sad love. At all events, her 'imaginism' allows her to ignore the objective fact that Jane's abilities shed a genuinely critical light upon her own limitations.

Frank Churchill plays along with Emma's conjecture, of course, and that further shores up her self-satisfaction. It gives her extra credit for perspicacity — at least, in her own eyes. Frank and Emma act out an effectively conspiratorial role. They cast themselves imaginatively as the two in the know, possessed of a shared 'intelligence' (chapter 26). For Emma, that gives them an advantage, not only over others, but over Jane herself. It makes Jane apparently a potential victim, unwittingly in their power, as, for instance, in chapter 28. Later, of course, when

Emma finally learns the truth, she will condemn Frank and Jane as having formed 'a league in secret to judge us all' (chapter 46). But Jane Austen means her words to have an ironic ring. As a comment on Frank and Jane's behaviour, they make comparatively little sense. But it is Emma herself who earlier formed a 'secret league' with Frank, and with motives that were similar to those she now attributes to Frank and Jane. There are other ironies here, too. Emma thinks Frank sees her as having come to some clever conclusions about Jane and Dixon. But actually, Frank has credited her with real powers of objective perception. He thinks she has surmised the objective truth about himself and Jane. Secondly, Emma supposes that it is she and Frank who are in the know, and keeping a secret. But in fact it's Frank and Jane. It is in this kind of way that, several times over, Jane Austen ironically undermines Emma's 'imaginism' — and not only her 'imaginism,' but the vanity to which it ministers.

The same irony constantly undercuts Emma's delusions about Frank, and his feelings for her. Jane Austen handles the irony with great subtlety here. Just before he leaves Highbury, for instance, Frank has an agitated interview with Emma, in which he almost tells her the truth:

> 'In short,' said he, 'perhaps, Miss Woodhouse — I think you can hardly be quite without suspicion' —
>
> He looked at her, as if wanting to read her thoughts. She hardly knew what to say. It seemed like the forerunner of something absolutely serious, which she did not wish.
>
> (chapter 30)

Because she doesn't 'wish' it, Emma stops Frank from going on. This is one of the finest moments in the novel. For Emma, the sense of her own power is apparently about to be consummated. She thinks Frank is on the point of telling her of his love for her. In fact, what Frank wants to tell her — that he and Jane are betrothed — would shatter the illusions of the 'imaginist' and deeply wound her vanity. But Jane Austen's finesse here lies, above all, in the fact that she makes Emma cut Frank short. For though the moment appears to consummate Emma's power, for her, it also represents the moment at which that imaginary power will have to end. If Frank tells her he loves her, she will have to admit that she doesn't love him. Then the hopes and illusions she imagines him as nursing will be at an end. But so will the flattery they offer her, and she wants that flattery to continue. So she cuts him off, and, at the same time, cuts herself off from the truth.

The scene is a marvellously ironic account of the mechanisms of a vain imagination at their most intricate. So, too, is the scene in which Emma meets Frank again, after his return to Highbury. Frank seems restless, and soon hurries away. Emma assumes that what she thinks of as his feelings for her are now less strong:

> She had no doubt as to his being less in love — but neither his agitated spirits, nor his hurrying away, seemed like a perfect cure; and she was rather inclined to think it implied a dread of her returning power, and a discreet resolution of not trusting himself with her long.

> (chapter 37)

In reality, of course, Frank's 'agitation' has nothing at all to do with Emma. He's 'hurrying away' to see Jane. The irony here is particularly fine in the contrast between the word 'dread' and the words 'rather inclined' and 'implied'. Actually, Emma wants to believe in her own irresistibility. But her intelligence is capable of scepticism, and it requires satisfaction, too. So she puts things in a way that is compatible with the demands of her intelligence. Actually, her vanity is imperious and intransigent. In the end, she believes what she wants to believe — believes in her 'power'. But she also feigns a certain reasonableness and detachment. In doing so, she effectively conceals her own motives from herself.

Of course, Emma's imagination also errs in leading her to assume that Harriet is attracted to Frank. She ends up making fanciful plans for Harriet to 'succeed' herself in Frank's 'affections' (chapter 31). Once again, the real point to those plans is a self-flattering one. Emma's acolyte and her admirer, joined together, not only in matrimony, but in a kind of society for the appreciation of Emma, as testimony to her power over others' lives, her ability to 'scheme' for their 'consolation and happiness' and 'comfort' — nothing could better please her vanity (chapter 31). But I want to dwell, now, on Emma's last mistake

— her suspicion that Knightley is falling in love with Harriet. Throughout the scene in which Knightley is trying to declare his love for her, Emma believes he is about to reveal his feelings for her protégé:

> 'Emma, I must tell what you will not ask, though I may wish it unsaid the next moment.'
> 'Oh! then, don't speak it, don't speak it,' she eagerly cried. 'Take a little time, consider, do not commit yourself.'
> 'Thank you,' said he, in an accent of deep mortification, and not another syllable followed.
>
> (chapter 49)

This scene ironically reverses the earlier scene with Frank. In the first, Emma imagines a declaration where one is not intended. Here, she imagines a confession of love for another woman where a declaration *is* intended. There is clearly a point both to the parallel and the reversal. For since the scene with Frank, Emma has recognised the mistakes she's made about Harriet, and Frank and Jane, too. She has been duly humbled, and has duly reproached herself. At the point when Knightley confesses his love, she is so chastened that she is almost more inclined to believe in Harriet's worth than her own. Her imagination is now at the service, not of vanity, but of self-reproach.

Before we assess the full significance of that change, it may be worth thinking back over what we've said so far. *Emma*, then, is an ironic and analytical study of the complex operations of vanity at its most subtle, and, in particular, of the way in which it uses imagination to obtain its ends. Emma is not crudely or ostentatiously vain. She doesn't praise herself in company, for example. She doesn't boast of her talents or acquaintance, in the way that Mrs Elton does (the contrast is part of the point to Mrs Elton's being there). Instead, Emma uses other people — and, more important, her imaginative apprehension of other people — to minister to her vanity. She creates images of other people that pander to her self-esteem. It may seem, however, at this point, that I've been rather too hard-headed about Emma, and rather too harsh on her. This might seem to be the more unfair, given Jane Austen's evident affection for her heroine. She thought that other people might not like Emma, but she knew that she herself did, and said so.

In any case, most readers have probably found Emma an attractive and sympathetic figure. Given my own argument, we might briefly wonder why.

The answer, I think, is that, essentially, Emma is endowed with good sense. Jane Austen means us to see her as having a natural affinity with the truth. It is only a temporary perversity that leads her astray. For Jane Austen, basically, Emma has the right kind of rational detachment from experience. It will ultimately make her capable of the kind of self-distrust that her creator sees as so desirable. In other words, Emma has the kind of intelligence that Jane Austen likes, but, for most of the novel, she misapplies it. Instead of using it to scrutinise herself and others as objectively as possible, she leaves it in thrall to her imagination and her vanity. She uses it to subtilise and refine her imaginative delusions. The scene in which she so completely misconstrues Frank's feelings for her is a good example of this process. So is the moment after Emma has read Frank's letter to Mrs Weston. The letter, of course, is full of praise for Emma herself:

> Gratifying, however, and stimulative as was the letter in the material part, its sentiments, she yet found, when it was folded up and returned to Mrs Weston, that it had not added any lasting warmth, that she could still do without the writer, and that he must learn to do without her.

(chapter 31)

The tone here could almost be Jane Austen's own. It is careful, controlled, measured, precise, discriminating and subtle. Its deliberation matches Emma's, of course. It has the methodical calm of a woman slowly folding a letter, and thinking out her own feelings as she does so. But all the thinking is based on absurd assumptions about her relationship with Frank, and Frank's feelings. This is typical of Emma. She is engaging and attractive partly because she is so often rather clever and so seldom very right. She is quite remarkable — perhaps unique, in fiction — in the particular ways in which she mixes intelligence and folly.

So, that Emma should progress towards self-distrust is crucially important, not least because it is a sign that she is beginning to apply what has always been the right kind of intelligence in the right way. Like Lizzie and Darcy in *Pride and Prejudice*, she learns the value of self-criticism, of not trusting subjective impressions, of a sceptical attitude to her own self. She comes to understand 'the deceptions' she has been 'practising on herself', the 'blunders, the blindness of her own head and heart' (chapter 47). She has been 'imposing on herself' to the most 'mortifying' degree (ibid.). 'To understand, thoroughly understand her own heart' becomes her 'first endeavour' (ibid.). In effect, Emma finally starts to recognise the value of the kind of intelligent self-awareness represented by Elinor Dashwood in *Sense and Sensibility*. She begins to learn the need to suspend both imagination and the workings of vanity in order precisely to see things as they are, objectively. It's partly this that makes her worthy of Knightley's hand at the end of the novel. For Knightley is far more capable than any other character of what is, for Jane Austen, a commendable objectivity. We should note here that Emma is not the only character in the novel who is guilty of 'imaginism', nor the only one who is prone to misconception. In fact, most of the characters make the same kind of mistake as Emma, but less often, and less dramatically. Mrs Weston, for instance, imagines that Knightley is attracted by Jane (chapter 26). Even without Emma's assistance, Harriet imagines that Knightley is attracted to her (chapter 47). Frank Churchill begins to imagine that Emma has guessed that truth about him and Jane (chapter 54). Jane imagines that Frank has started to fall in love with Emma (chapter 47). The reasons for others' misunderstandings are never quite the same as Emma's. But, during the course of the novel, the misunderstandings none the less proliferate.

The difficulties of escaping from subjective vision, and of attaining true, objective knowledge are always likely to hamper any given character. In Jane Austen's terms, objectivity is not easily attained, and never wholly or securely attained. Knightley himself does not always grasp matters correctly. He mistakenly imagines, for instance, that Emma is falling in love with Frank. But, on the other hand, it is Knightley alone who is perceptive enough to suspect something of the liaison — 'private liking ... private understanding, even' — between Churchill and Jane. In fact, chapter 41 gives us a precise sense of the difference, in this kind of respect, between him and the other characters, especially Emma. Though suspecting the truth about Jane and Frank, he questions his own suspicions, and the observations on which they're based. He is sceptical about his own deductions. He's anxious to escape Emma's 'errors of imagination'. He is wary of being 'like Cowper and his fire at twilight. "Myself creating what I saw"'. Knightley is fallible and liable to error. The difference is that he knows it. He is therefore ready to doubt his own judgement. He has that power of detachment from self, of self-criticism, which is vital to any approach to objective perception. Only when Emma realises that she has been 'creating what she sees' herself — only when she is on her guard against doing so — can she become a fit partner for Knightley. Only then can she relinquish 'imaginism' for objectivity.

AFTERTHOUGHTS

1

Explain Gibson's references to Don Quixote in his opening paragraph.

2

Do you agree that Emma's behaviour towards Harriet is 'essentially self-interested' (page 70)?

3

What different aspects of vanity are highlighted in this essay?

4

Do you feel that Emma has gained when 'she can relinquish "imaginism" for objectivity' (final paragraph)?

Graham Holderness

Graham Holderness is Head of the Drama department at the Roehampton Institute of Higher Education, and has published numerous books and critical articles.

ESSAY

Disliking the heroine in *Emma*

If we attempted to define the self-evident characteristics of Jane Austen's art of fiction, the list of qualities would include: realism or naturalism; irony and humour; and the ethical and educational impulses of a moralist. We tend to assume a natural and easy relationship between these separate elements; and we tend to think of Jane Austen's novels in particular as perfectly homogeneous integrations of whatever diverse materials they assimilate, exquisitely crafted objects carved into a sculptured unity from her 'two inches of ivory'. But the relationships between the different perspectives — realist, humorous-ironic and moralistic — on which the novels draw, may on further investigation prove to be more problematical than we imagine.

The obvious complication in our reading of such fiction is the fact that these different perspectives frequently call for different kinds of response and interpretation, even for the same character or scene. The conventions of realism encourage us to focus our attention on what is normal, common, everyday in the life of a society — where exceptional events occur, they are in any case recognisable as natural developments of that society — and to adopt in our interpretations of the fictional universe standards of judgement and expectations of behaviour similar to those which operate in our everyday lives. Humour on the other hand delights in the unusual, the incongruous, the absurd, and involves a suspension of the constraints of everyday judgement: we may laugh at what in other circumstances or in reality we might experience as distressing, or terrifying, or shameful.

The ironist and the moralist are frequently to be found in the same artistic consciousness, and some of the greatest ironists, such as Swift, have exemplified both: the purpose of irony's incongruous juxtapositions may be to produce the savage indignation that can lacerate the follies and absurdities of the age. Yet the essence of moralistic writing is that the reader should know where he or she stands, should be able to orientate his or her responses within a clear and guaranteed moral framework, should know exactly what or who is right or wrong; while the essence of ironical writing is that the writer is not quite saying exactly what he or she means, and may indeed be implying the very opposite of the text's apparent surface meaning. The doubleness of ironical writing, the distance it sustains between what is said and what is meant, makes it a far more intangible and elusive mode of communication than the necessarily clear and sharp antitheses of a moralistic perspective.

Some of the critical problems that are at the heart of our readings of *Emma* may lie along the spliced rope of these diversified strands; in particular that tantalising reference of the author's to 'a heroine whom no one would like but myself', which seems to throw our categories into contradictory juxtaposition. Was Austen confessing to a *humorous* approach to a character she expected most of her readers to respond to in terms of the sober responsibilities of *realism*? Was she adopting an *ironical* perspective where others would wish to *moralise*? And what implications does this enigma have for our reading of the novel? Does the heroine, sharply illuminated by the searching lights of realism and morality, remain 'dislikeable'; or has the novelist reserved to herself, somewhere in the corridors of the text, an illumination of a different kind: an amused an ironical consciousness not only of her heroine, but of the impact that Emma could be envisaged making on her readers — a consciousness that might be glimpsed filtering through the doorways of the closed Regency drawing-room, and casting an alternative light across her rational and naturalistic drama of domestic manners?

Let us consider, as an illustration of the interaction of these different elements of Austen's fiction, the episode in chapter 43, in which Emma offends Miss Bates on Box Hill. The incident of the insult itself is very briefly dramatised, and can be quoted as a whole:

'It will not do', whispered Frank to Emma . . . 'I am ordered by Miss Woodhouse to say . . . she only demands from each of you either one thing very clever, be it prose or verse, original or repeated — or two things moderately clever — or three things very dull indeed, and she engages to laugh heartily at them all.'

'Oh! very well', exclaimed Miss Bates, 'then I need not be uneasy. "Three things very dull indeed." That will just do for me, you know, I shall be sure to say three dull things as soon as ever I open my mouth, shan't I? — (looking round with the most good-humoured dependence on every body's assent) — Do not you all think I shall?

Emma could not resist.

'Ah! ma'am, but there may be a difficulty. Pardon me — but you will be limited as to number — only three at once.'

Miss Bates, deceived by the mock ceremony of her manner, did not immediately catch her meaning; but when it burst on her, it could not anger, though a slight blush showed that it could pain her.

'Ah! — well — to be sure. Yes, I see what she means (turning to Mr Knightley,) and I will try to hold my tongue. I must make myself very disagreeable, or she would not have said such a thing to an old friend.'

Considered firstly as a realistic portrayal of a credible episode in the developing social and personal relationships of a small group of Regency gentry, this episode displays features typical of Austen's art: though the setting is a picnic at a favoured leisure spot, the narrative consists almost entirely of dialogue, and 'Box Hill' has as little concrete reality as a piece of pictorial scenery in a naturalistic stage-set.

Seven miles were travelled in expectation of enjoyment, and every body had a burst of admiration on first arriving

Not a word of descriptive detail (if we except the formal phrase 'beautiful views' that occurs later in the chapter) is supplied to embody for the reader any concrete physical stimulus for these responses. 'Reality' for Jane Austen consisted primarily of the verbal and gestural medium of communication between her characters: there is none of the interdependence and interaction between character and environment that we find in, for example, Thomas Hardy's fiction. What happens at Box Hill could easily be conceived as happening on the pier at Brighton, or among the teacups at Bath. This characteristic feature of the fiction carries important implications: since our understanding and interpretation of what 'happens' depends entirely on our reading of the complex and elaborate codes of a society's communicative discourse. When a character in a Thomas Hardy novel is seduced, or rejected, or abandoned, the landscape itself changes colour and appearance: the nature of 'reality' assumes a different shape. Emma insults Miss Bates, offends Mr Knightley, and ends up disgusted with herself: but Box Hill is not altered by the action; what happens happens within the language-world that binds and contains the characters' relationships with one another and with their society, and whatever changes occur as a consequence are registered there. A picnic party begins with the vocabulary of lively and light-hearted social intercourse (I have italicised the relevant words):

> ... Frank Churchill grew *talkative* and *gay*, making her his first object. Every distinguishing *attention* that could be paid, was paid to her. To *amuse* her, and be *agreeable* in her eyes, seemed all that he cared for — and Emma, *glad* to be *enlivened*, not sorry to be *flattered*, was *gay* and *easy* too ...

And ends in the language of humiliation, mortification and self-disgust:

> Never had she felt so *agitated, mortified, grieved*, at any circumstance in her life. She was most *forcibly struck*. The truth of his representation there was no denying. She felt it at her heart. How could she have been so *brutal*, so *cruel* to Miss Bates! — How could she have exposed herself to such *ill opinion* in any one she valued!

Such revelations of relationship and psychological development are easily intelligible if language is, as Jane Austen's eighteenth-century predecessors thought it was, a clear, reliable and luminous representation of reality. But Jane Austen lived between two ages, the rationalistic world of eighteenth-century philosophy and the rapidly changing, unsettled world of the romantic poets: she lived at the same time as William Blake. We cannot simply assume that she regarded language, as John Locke did, as a transparent window onto reality. It was also open to her to draw from and participate in the new kinds of awareness that were developing in European culture under the impact of the great historical changes of the age; so it remains for us to prove whether or not language figures in her novels as a trustworthy guide to the world, or as a complex system of devices for constructing, representing and misrepresenting the nature of reality.

I will concentrate next on moralistic interpretation of this episode, since that is probably the most familiar perspective applied to it in criticism and teaching. We do not have to search very far to find an authoritative moral judgement of Emma's conduct and of the wider significance of the episode itself: since such an ethical interpretation is to be found ready-made in Mr Knightley's searing rebuke:

> Emma, I must once more speak to you as I have been used to do: a privilege rather endured than allowed, perhaps, but I must still use it. I cannot see you acting wrong, without a remonstrance. How could you be so unfeeling to Miss Bates? How could you be so insolent in your wit to a woman of her character, age, and situation? — Emma, I had not thought it possible.

Mr Knightley applies to Emma's behaviour a clear and unequivocal standard of moral judgement: she has been 'acting wrong'. (Mr Knightley is not guilty here of grammatical irregularity: by 'acting' he means 'enacting', and 'wrong' is a noun, not a truncated adverb.) A 'remonstrance' is not simply a proffered ethical judgement, or a formulation of moral instruction: it is both a demonstration and an appeal, an attempt to show someone the error of their ways in a spirit of engaged solicitude and shared responsibility — an attempt to persuade by reason and example, rather than to control by discipline and force.

The specific charges are allegations of insolence, insensitivity, and the unworthy and irresponsible employment of cleverness against an easy victim. We could easily universalise this dramatised situation by finding possible parallel examples of youth mocking old age, sophistication insulting naïveté. But like all moral judgements, Mr Knightley's is not in any sense absolute: it is dependent on the particular conventions of a specific society. He himself makes that clear by detailing ('character, age and situation') the precise violations of social convention and moral code that Emma is accused of committing. It is wrong, in Mr Knightley's eyes, for a young woman (to use the terms of Jane Austen's world) of birth, education and fortune to take advantage of a woman who is self-evidently her inferior in all three. Miss Bates's age, poverty and dependence should make her an object of 'compassion' (chapter 43) to a sensitive and responsible occupant of Emma's social position.

It would therefore be quite misleading to try to understand this incident by hypothesising comparable examples: how you would feel, for instance, if you had yielded to the temptation to mock an elderly and boring relative at a family party, and received in turn a remonstrance from someone whose judgement you admired and whose opinion you valued. Although the terms Mr Knightley uses are not at all impersonal, the basis of his rebuke is an ideology of *noblesse oblige*; a clear conception not only of what is appropriate to Emma's personal circumstances, but of the moral responsibilities entailed with the privileges of her social position. Had the same words been spoken to a social equal (to Mrs Elton, perhaps) he would not have regarded them as an abuse of the freedoms of conversation — 'Were she a woman of fortune ... I would not quarrel with you for any liberties of manner' (chapter 43). It is precisely because she has the advantages of wealth and education that Emma should observe moral conventions, that what is right in ethical terms accords exactly with what is socially fitting and proper. Mr Knightley's sentiments may be mistaken for the accents of modern democracy, but they represent in fact the exact opposite: they belong to the ideology of an old aristocracy, scrupulously and punctiliously stipulating the responsibility of power and wealth to offer protection and alleviation to weakness and poverty; they are in reality no more democratic than Emma's aspirations to elevate Harriet Smith can be considered early examples of socialist egalitarianism.

None the less, whatever qualifications we may wish to offer, the moralistic interpretation proposed by the narrative is clear and definitive; and insofar as Mr Knightley is presented as a figure of moral authority and a source of ethical wisdom (about which more below) his judgement will stand as a valid moral analysis. Given that Emma takes his judgement completely to heart and rebukes herself in analogous terms, there seems to be little necessity to question Mr Knightley's wisdom. If we combine what has already been said about 'realism' with a positive evaluation of Knightley's morality, then we could argue convincingly that the true object of Jane Austen's realism, couched in her dramatisation of a society's world of language, is the moral content of her characters' relationships; and that between them the narrator and the leading male character supply all the linguistic exactness and moral clarity required for the reader to find orientation within the artistic and ethical universe of the novel.

What has happened, meantime, to our category of humour? Where, in the stern sobriety of these judgements about conduct and propriety, do we find anything to amuse? It is dangerously easy to assume that Jane Austen's techniques of ironical presentation and humorous observation simply go into suspension when her fiction addresses matters of gravity or serious import. And it is certainly not always easy to see how the strenuous moral earnestness we have been taught to expect from serious fiction can co-exist with the moral subversiveness of humour. We might well deduce, from what has been said so far, that the narrative endorses this assumption by making Emma's attempt at humorous verbal play the occasion of a moral and emotional crisis. A joke is always at someone's expense: it invites, from one party, participation in the complicity of laughter; and excludes a third party from that compact of amusement, isolating him or her or them as objects of a mockery perceived but not shared. The structure of Emma's humour assimilates Frank Churchill into a conspiracy of cleverness, and isolates Miss Bates into an object of ridicule.

The forbidding tones of moral castigation should not however induce us to forget the kinds of humorous awareness fostered by the narrative itself. How, for example, is Miss Bates presented in the general body of the narrative? Has the novelist been using her formidable privilege and power, liberty of speech and authority of opinion, in a manner appropriate to her position, to protect the weak and to engender compassion for the innocent? Jane Austen's writing seems an antithesis of the sentimental romance which would be the appropriate vehicle for communicating such a perspective: its delight in the ridiculous, the absurd, the comic, is never constrained by such sensitivities. The presentation of Miss Bates throughout the novel is precisely such as to encourage the reader to share Emma's sense of both her absurdity and her irksomeness. The kind of witticism prac- tised by Emma on the tedious spinster is exactly the kind of humorous mockery brought into play every time Miss Bates enters the narrative: every rambling monologue assigned to the character confirms that she could never remain content with saying only three dull things at once. There is almost a sense of injustice in the novelist's arrogation of complete liberty to ridicule the old and silly, while her heroine receives a short sharp shock of punishment for practising the same licence; a sense of unfairness that a narrator can preserve to herself such immunity from moral prosecution, while her character is criti- cised for deploying precisely the same verbal and imaginative freedoms.

The dramatisation of the offence seems also to contain a remarkable critique of irony itself:

> Miss Bates, deceived by the mock ceremony of her manner, did not immediately catch her meaning . . .

> (chapter 43)

'Mock ceremony' would be an excellent description of Jane Austen's own irony. Emma is here, in other words, employing that very technique of ironical equivocation that we would regard as a key constitutive element of Jane Austen's art. One example will suffice — the narrator's account of Mrs Churchill's death:

> Goldsmith tells us, that when lovely woman stoops to folly, she has nothing to do but to die; and when she stoops to be dis- agreeable, it is equally to be recommended as a clearer of ill-

fame. Mrs Churchill, after being disliked at least twenty-five years, was now spoken of with compassionate allowances. In one point she was fully justified. She had never been admitted before to be seriously ill. The event acquitted her of all the fancifulness, and all the selfishness of imaginary complaints.

(chapter 45)

There is no need to speculate about how thoroughly deceived Miss Bates would be by the 'mock ceremony' of the author's manner in this passage, since the Miss Bateses of the world were clearly never seriously considered as potential readers of the novel. But how could Jane Austen have been so brutal, so cruel to Mrs Churchill? How could she be so insolent in her wit to a woman of her character, age and situation? The effective invisibility of the character, who never appears *in propria persona*, is clearly a kind of explanation of the novelist's singular lack of restraint in abusing her: though not an entirely adequate one, since the choice of extending or withholding sympathy lies within the writer's prerogative. The cruel relish of irony in exposing human absurdity here flourishes quite free from the constraints of realism or the sanctions of morality: there is no Mr Knightley to curb with the lash of remonstrance the uninhibited liberty of Jane Austen's wit and imagination.

When we examine the effects of these three different perspectives, they cannot be regarded as wholly compatible with one another. Irony and humour are at odds with both realism and morality: so the reader is effectively being offered different and perhaps incompatible signals, persuaded towards different and even contradictory interpretations. If we accept that the object of Jane Austen's realistic presentation is the 'discourse' of her characters' communications, then our only clues to the reality of what has 'happened' lie within language itself — within a medium of signs rendered elusive and unstable by the presence of irony. Supported by clear definitions of moral convention, we could accept Emma's insult to Miss Bates, however trivial it may appear to be, as an offence of some gravity and seriousness. But once those clear definitions are subjected to any kind of questioning or challenge — by for example an ironical doubleness in the narrative itself, or by a detached awareness of historical relativity — then the offence could swell into grandeur or dwindle into insignificance, depending on the perspective of interpretation. If the reader has been encouraged to regard a character as a tedious bore, appropriately ridiculed by an ironist's humour, then the sudden wrist-slap of a moralistic intrusion may well seem too abrupt a shift of perspective, too substantial a pill to swallow at one gulp.

A simpler way of putting the problem would be to ask: which of these perspectives seems to represent most accurately the overall 'point of view' of the novelist? Many would argue that Austen's position was in effect that of Mr Knightley, and that the novel chronicles the heroine's gradual conversion to the truth and wisdom he represents. Yet clearly the novel is no simple moral fable, no crude exposition of dogmatic Knightleyism. Emma herself shares some of the novelist's qualities of wit, sophisticated irony and imaginative freedom: in a famous and much-quoted passage (chapter 39), Austen refers to her heroine as an 'imaginist' — one who tries to re-create and control the world by the power of fantasy. The definition may well be double-edged: Emma certainly fails to change or even influence her world by the exercise of her imagination. But without the liberating potentialities of imagination, the fictitious world of the novel could never have been created in the first place. Mr Knightley's moralism demands that Emma should sacrifice those qualities to the requirements of a rigorous ethical code; but surely the novelist is not voluntarily surrendering those qualities from herself? Is the uninhibited fearless liveliness of the heroine's imagination a surer indication of where the novelist's sympathies lay?

If there is a consistently sustained ironic perspective permeating the whole novel, then it will inevitably be larger and more inclusive than either Knightley's ethical severity or Emma's imaginative liberty. The amused ironical consciousness of the narrator could observe the conflict of these opposites from a more remote and detached position, requiring commitment to neither side. Both Emma and Knightley are viewed, as they enact their respective roles in the Box Hill incident, with some ironic amusement. Knightley's recourse to a sermon on the social importance of charity clearly exposes the class basis of his ethical ideology; and Emma's obvious concern with the personality of the moralist over and above the application of his moralising betrays that her respect for Mr Knightley's judgement depends on certain unconscious impulses that only later come to light: 'How could she have exposed herself to such ill opinion in any one she valued! And how suffer him to leave her without saying one word of gratitude, of concurrence, of common kindness!' (chapter 43). For if there is one blind spot in Emma's deluded imagination that is clearly visible to the reader, it is that this strong-willed daughter of a weak-willed father will eventually reconcile her will to the patriarchal authority of the man who appoints himself her moral guide. As Knightley expounds the responsibilities of the aristocracy and Emma reflects on the offence she has caused him, poor old Miss Bates fades even more completely into the background.

What Emma and Knightley have in common, despite the ritualised conflicts and trials they enact and undergo, is a deeply conservative pride in their own class and the value of their own position within it: the ground of their compatibility, beyond all the moral struggles and emotional conflicts, is a deeply rooted reciprocal reverence for social convention. If we remain sensitive to the possibilities of irony and doubleness, mockery and humour in the narrative, we need not be bound by the assumption that Austen was directly promulgating moral ideas through the opinions of her characters. Mr Knightley may be presented with as much detachment, and as little encouragement for us to endorse his views, as Emma is herself.

I do not believe that Jane Austen did 'like' her heroine in any of the usual senses; but neither can she be inferred to have 'liked' her hero. What she probably 'liked' was the effect that the interrelationships of hero and heroine would have on her readers; not least in terms of the ambivalent doubleness of an ironical narrative with the power temporarily to liberate both writer and readers from the chafing burden of class-based morality and social convention.

AFTERTHOUGHTS

1

Explain Holderness's reference to 'two inches of ivory' in his opening paragraph.

2

Do you agree that what happens at Box Hill 'could easily be conceived as happening on the pier at Brighton' (page 84)?

3

How can one tell when reading *Emma* whether or not a statement is ironic?

4

Does Holderness convince you that 'Jane Austen did not "like" her heroine in any of the usual senses' (final paragraph)?

Christopher Turner

Christopher Turner is Director of Studies for English and the Performing Arts at Cheadle Hulme High School. He has edited Huckleberry Finn *for Longman Study Texts.*

ESSAY

Aspects of comedy in *Emma*

Comedy can range from savage satire to light entertainment; its tone can reflect a certain cynicism, as well as — more characteristically — an optimistic perspective on life that suggests that problems can be resolved and misunderstandings corrected; and its subject can range from the fantastic to the familiar world of everyday life, conversations, love affairs and marriage. Marriage, indeed, is very often a component of comedy. Not only can courtship and marriage be themselves the focus of much humour, but many comedies (Shakespeare's, for example) traditionally depend on a comic pattern whereby the play's or story's action is concluded by a marriage (or — more often — a group of marriages) as a signal that reconciliations and understandings have been achieved and that future happiness is assured. This essay will seek to examine *Emma* in the context of these traditions. But more specifically, I shall be seeking to establish in my analysis the sheer *range* of comic effects that the novel has to offer.

Novelists choose their characters' names with great care, and Jane Austen is no exception. Mr Woodhouse, for all his wealth and social status is essentially a static and rather wooden character; Harriet Smith is as ordinary as her surname implies; Miss Bates is annoying and eventually exasperates ('baits') Emma into a stinging riposte; Mrs Augusta Elton has all the grandiose self-importance and pretentiousness that her Christian name suggests.

At first sight, then, the above seem unlikely material for comedy, but as these characters appear before us, we see the importance of *how* they are presented as well as *what* they are. Mr Woodhouse hates change, he is fussy, and his fixations about people catching cold and the beneficial effects of thin gruel become running jokes throughout the novel. He represents a recognisable comic type, that of the 'old buffer' who stands in the way of progress and clings tenaciously to 'the old ways'.

However, Emma tolerates him and respects him; he allows her to be the mistress of his house while she respects his overall authority. Furthermore, when Jane Austen achieves humour at his expense, it is gently done; his over-solicitous concern for Mrs Bates's diet at the end of chapter 3 is a typical example, as is the author's comment:

> Emma allowed her father to talk . . .

It is that kind of comment which allows us to see Mr Woodhouse for what he is: a representative of that seemingly inevitable conservatism of the aged, which, however, always leaves us smiling, never castigating.

Miss Bates is much more infuriating. As a type, she is the vacuous chatterbox, filling her empty life with empty conversation. Jane Austen allows her to talk *at* us, invariably without further comment, trusting us to see her as Emma does. At the ball in chapter 38 there is a fine example of Miss Bates in full flow, pointedly prefaced with the comment:

> . . . every body's words were soon lost under the incessant flow of Miss Bates, who came in talking, and had not finished her speech under many minutes after her being admitted into the circle at the fire.

She is treated as a charity case, someone on the fringes of 'life as it is really lived', someone who is to be tolerated for the good of one's soul, but who is, nevertheless, annoying and a strain on one's good temper. It is, therefore, a masterly inversion of our reactions to her that Jane Austen uses this figure of fun as a catalyst at a crucial stage in the process of Emma's maturation; suddenly our hearts go out to her at Box Hill in chapter 43, when Emma causes Miss Bates pain by not resisting the opportunity for a jibe at her dullness of chatter, and we are made to feel *our* sniggering sense of superiority vanish, just as Emma's does.

Augusta Elton is quite different. She represents the 'new arrival' who immediately takes charge in defiance of the established pecking order. Jane Austen allows Mrs Elton to reveal herself through her chatter, but the novelist also makes very clear her contempt for her through dismissive, concise comment; for example, in chapter 34, Mrs Elton is described as being 'as elegant as lace and pearls could make her', implying that however fine and fashionable the externals might be, they are still not enough to redeem the whole person. Repeated references to Maple Grove are her hallmark, but perhaps more crucial to her function as a caricature is her lack of development as a character. On hearing that Mr Knightley and Emma are to live with her father after their marriage, Mrs Elton remarks at the end of chapter 53:

> Shocking plan, living together. It would never do. She knew a family near Maple Grove who had tried it, and been obliged to separate before the end of the first quarter.

Her blinkered, unchanging perspective, as revealed above, makes her a universal figure of fun, the kind of character we feel no qualms about ridiculing.

Those are the main comic caricatures of the novel, all based on recognisable and well-used types, yet each endowed with individuality. They all share the characteristic of hardly changing throughout the novel: Mr Woodhouse, for example, cannot conceive why Mr Knightley and Emma should change the basis of their relationship by getting married, saying in chapter 53, 'Why could they not go on as they had done?'.

But what of Emma herself? From one perspective, she is unlikely material for a comic role — she is egotistical, arrogant, full of her own importance, devious, and has a tendency to see people in general, and Harriet in particular, as 'things' to be moved around and orchestrated much as one might use chess pieces (see her reference, in the second paragraph of chapter 4, to Harriet as 'something which her home required').

However, it is possible to cast her in the role of the comic heroine, experiencing the traditional series of trials and tribulations before achieving happiness with the right man. What makes Emma different as a comic heroine is that she is the creator and perpetrator of her own predicaments; what makes her additionally special is that we see her mature and change radically during the novel, so that our reactions to her are constantly changing.

Emma is endearing from the beginning because of her capacity for laughter; there are many occasions when she withdraws from a scene to laugh in secret at a character or at what has been said. She is keenly aware of the humorous potential in so many of life's trying moments; in addition, she sees humour's usefulness as a way of coping with criticism, self-doubt, and disappointment.

Furthermore, we see in Emma the potential of humour as a sophisticated weapon for the exposure of human foolishness; she uses it to criticise others, both openly and to herself, but also, and this is the fascinating aspect of her personality, she uses it to reveal her own weaknesses to herself.

Certainly, Emma is solicitous in her attentions to those less fortunate than herself; however, she is never sentimental about her charitable visits, and she is at pains to disabuse herself of notions of altruism. In chapter 10, she and Harriet have been paying a charitable visit to an impoverished family living on the outskirts of Highbury, and on their way home, Emma has this to say:

> These are the sights, Harriet, to do one good. How trifling they make every thing else appear! — I feel now as if I could think of nothing but these poor creatures all the rest of the day; and yet, who can say how soon it may all vanish from my mind?

The mock pomposity followed by the revelation of such self-knowledge is refreshing and endearing.

The growth of the individual towards greater self-knowledge is one of the central issues of the novel, and its most dramatic manifestation is Emma herself. One key aspect is the ability to laugh at oneself, and Emma reveals that capacity fairly early in the novel, thus giving us grounds for hope that she will ultimately succeed in gaining a greater measure of self-awareness. Towards the end of chapter 16, Emma is thinking aloud to herself about her attempts to make a match for Harriet. She realises it was mistaken, and that she must stop it, but almost immediately starts casting around for another suitor for Harriet:

> She stopt to blush and laugh at her own relapse, and then resumed a more serious, more dispiriting cogitation upon what had been, and might be, and must be.

At the end of the novel, Emma finds herself having to adjust her previous opposition to the idea of marrying Mr Knightley. As she thinks about her nephew Henry losing his inheritance of Donwell Abbey, she muses:

> Think she must of the possible difference to the poor little boy; and yet she only gave herself a saucy conscious smile about it, and found amusement in detecting the real cause of that violent dislike of Mr Knightley's marrying Jane Fairfax, or any body else . . .
>
> (chapter 51)

That kind of self-knowledge allows the individual to laugh at past follies, to smile at the accommodations of the present, and still command admiration and respect — a very healthy stance, and one entirely in keeping with the great tradition of literary comedy.

A hallmark of Austen's style is her varied deployment of irony: the humorous use of language where words imply the opposite of what they normally mean. It is also possible to refer to 'irony of situation', where there is a mismatch between what is expected to happen and what actually transpires.

Irony depends on the reader or viewer being aware of incongruity, and for it to be effective the user of irony must give enough clear signs of its presence. Irony, therefore, can be as much about the tone of the language as about the actual words themselves. Austen's irony is special because it is the literary device that best suits one of her main purposes in writing, which is the examination of character; ironic language has a surface meaning and a different, deeper meaning, just as people have a superficial, public presentation of themselves, as well as deeper, more private aspects. Both unconsciously ironic revelations from characters and deliberately ironic authorial intrusions help us to understand and make judgements about characters.

Irony enables us, therefore, to remain distant from some characters and to criticise them more easily, but paradoxically it also enables us to draw closer to others, as the less attractive veneer is stripped away, and the finer qualities, kept scrupulously hidden, are revealed in all their glory.

Irony can be gentle, with the result that we can feel superior to characters without damning them completely. Consider the novelist's cameo of Mrs Bates at the beginning of chapter 3:

> Mrs Bates, the widow of a former vicar of Highbury, was a very old lady, almost past every thing but tea and quadrille. She lived with her single daughter in a very small way, and was considered with all the regard and respect which a harmless old lady, under such untoward circumstances, can excite.

There is nothing there to cause offence, yet the barbs are apparent; consider the choice of 'excite', and the comment about being 'almost past every thing'.

Miss Bates comes in for similar treatment a little later in the same chapter:

> She was a great talker upon little matters, which exactly suited Mr Woodhouse, full of trivial communications and harmless gossip.

Note the contrast of 'great' and 'little', the mild criticism of Mr Woodhouse's fondness for trivia, and the reminder that it is all 'harmless' anyway. The irony here enables us to stand back from these characters, see them as the light-weights they are; yet never are we expected to disparage them.

Jane Austen uses the irony of understatement very effectively, particularly when interpreting for us the reactions of characters. In chapter 21, Jane Fairfax is in conversation with an animated Miss Bates about the arrival of Mr Elton's new wife at the vicarage, but Jane is less than excited about the news:

> Jane's curiosity did not appear of that absorbing nature as wholly to occupy her.

This authorial comment amuses us, as we are allowed to share

Jane's thoughts, and learn that she is bored. It also sets the mood of slightly forced politeness for the rest of the conversation. Such is the power of the well-chosen ironic intrusion.

Authorial irony is important in directing our thinking about certain characters. It also amuses us, and enables us to feel superior. However, when we turn to Emma, we see a further layer of complexity, because Emma can be ironic to herself about herself.

The opening paragraph of chapter 31 will serve admirably to illustrate the point. Jane is considering the nature of her feelings for Frank Churchill. The first two sentences are highly effective in establishing the twin viewpoints of high seriousness and ironic self-deprecation:

> Emma continued to entertain no doubt of her being in love. Her ideas only varied as to how much.

From then on, there is a debate taking place as Emma vainly tries to apply a rational approach to an emotional situation, with the result that, by the end of the paragraph, she has almost convinced herself that she cannot be in love at all because:

> . . . a strong attachment certainly must produce more of a struggle than she could foresee in her own feelings.

That bathetic descent from being sure about her feelings to an almost despairing realisation that she might be deluding herself is done with an awareness of the essential irony of attempting to apply logic to sentiments, but also with the revelation that Emma is as prone to insecurity and emotional confusion as the rest of us, and that her wit and intelligence are of little use in an aspect of her life where experience and wisdom are singularly lacking — in other words, we see her weaknesses exposed in the withering glare of self-revelation.

The overall effect, though, is to evoke sympathy for one so sure on the outside, yet so confused and insecure on the inside. Irony, bathos, self-deception, and attempts to convince herself all play their parts in showing us just what condition Emma is in. We are brought closer to her, not just because we are privy to those thoughts, but because of the ways in which they are presented to us. The style goes hand in hand with the content.

Another important aspect of the tradition of comedy is its

visual appeal. It is a feature of Jane Austen's writing that she employs the 'set piece' for that purpose. Not only does such an occasion add a more prominent and visually appealing backdrop to the proceedings, it also provides the perfect opportunity for character, style, and thematic interaction to be seen at its best.

There are a number of such moments in *Emma*, each worthy of the closest examination: there is Mr Elton's proposal to Emma in the carriage, the incident with the gipsies and its aftermath, the ball, and, supremely, Box Hill. But let us take the incident of the painting of Harriet's portrait in chapter 6, for there we have an early example, not just of visual comedy, but also of that special blend of literary qualities that Jane Austen employs at such moments.

At this stage of the novel, Emma is convinced that her plans to match Harriet with Mr Elton are going very well. Emma's suggestion that Harriet 'have your likeness taken' is greeted with great enthusiasm by Mr Elton, and so the painting is duly completed.

A painting is a visual representation of reality as the artist sees it; it can be said that literature performs much the same function, using words. In this incident, then, the author is not only presenting characters to us in a precise setting and focusing their and our attention on a limited range of events, but she is also examining the basis on which we make assumptions and deductions about what we regard as being 'real' and 'true'.

The language of the opening pages of this chapter is consciously artistic, more akin to sculpture than painting, but nevertheless closely allied to the concept of construing reality: Mr Elton praises Emma for 'the attractions you have added' to Harriet, and he states, 'Skilful has been the hand'. The notion of Harriet being clay in the hands of Emma is further enhanced by this comment from Mr Elton:

> She was a beautiful creature when she came to you, but, in my opinion, the attractions you have added are infinitely superior to what she received from nature.

Emma is aware of an element of flattery in Mr Elton's praise for her paintings, which provides an opportunity for one of those typical moments of insight into Emma's thinking:

Don't pretend to be in raptures about mine. Keep your raptures for Harriet's face.

After so much praise, it comes as a delightfully amusing surprise to discover that Emma's paintings have their limitations, and this is where irony comes into its own.

The description of Emma's portfolio ('not one of [the portraits] had ever been finished') is the occasion for gentle mockery, but also for a more general appreciation of Emma's weaknesses, so that the particular expands into the general:

> She had always wanted to do everything ... but steadiness had always been wanting; and in nothing had she approached the degree of excellence which she would have been glad to command, and ought not to have failed of.

That is hardly an auspicious augury at the start of a portrait-painting session, not to mention at a well-advanced stage of an attempt to control the destinies of two people.

Jane Austen seizes the chance for intrusions to guide our awareness and our thinking, as, using typical irony, she states:

> There was merit in every drawing — in the least finished, perhaps the most ...

One of the great advantages of the 'set piece' is that it allows characters to react to an external, so that we can see aspects of characters in relation to that external, and not solely in relation to each other.

This episode is no exception, as it brings together Mr Elton, Mr Knightley, Mr Woodhouse and Emma in front of the likeness of Harriet Smith. Mr Elton pronounces it 'a most perfect resemblance in every feature'; Mr Knightley says, 'You have made her too tall'; Emma has to admit to herself that he is right, but she is not prepared to agree openly, so stays silent; Mr Woodhouse is more concerned 'that she seems to be sitting out of doors, with only a little shawl over her shoulders — and it makes one think she must catch cold'.

What an effective way to facilitate character revelation. Mr Elton is clearly besotted (with Emma), so everything she does must be wonderful; Mr Knightley further enhances his role as the truth-teller; Emma reveals to us her ability to acknowledge the truth at the same time as she conspires to present a façade; Mr Woodhouse is so blinkered by his obsessions that he worries about the future health of a person in a painting.

This particular episode establishes at a comparatively early stage in the novel the thematic importance of the ability to make judgements on the evidence of perceptions of what we take to be the reality of a person, a relationship, an emotion, or whatever else we regard as being a trustworthy indicator, even if sometimes it happens to be a painting.

Such moments, then, reveal the complex intertwining of the strands of the novelist's art, with the result that we have a vivid awareness of the scene, the characters, and the emergence of themes, communicated to us through the medium of a range of stylistic effects.

Turning now to the finale, the ending of a comedy is crucial, for it is the long-expected moment of resolution, when problems are sorted out, friendships renewed, marriages made, and tensions eased. The denouement is crucial for its assertion of those optimistic values and attitudes which are the foundations of the comic view of life.

However, it is the moment when 'true' comedy can lapse into 'sentimental' comedy, when the paper tissue assumes greater importance than the wry, thoughtful, appreciative smile. The great comic writers (and dramatists) avoid that descent by leaving you with hopes raised that, despite the problems (and some of them may still be around), there is hope for the achievement of human happiness.

Often the resolution of problems is assisted by the unexpected intervention of someone or something from outside, the *deus ex machina* concept of classical drama. It reminds us that, despite our rational and analytical skills, we often need the unforeseen to help us towards success.

At the end of *Emma*, Jane Austen has two problems to solve: the continued opposition of Mr Woodhouse to the proposed marriage of Mr Knightley and Emma, and how to avoid a sentimental, fairy-tale ending. With the first, she resorts to the tradition of comedy, and with the second, she trusts in her ability to use her particular story-telling and stylistic techniques to complement her reliance on the comic tradition.

Mr Woodhouse is won over because Mrs Weston's turkeys

were stolen one night, 'evidently by the ingenuity of man', therefore it seems to be a good idea to have a man about the place for protection, of life, property, and, presumably, turkeys — and so the marriage can go ahead. Once again we see Jane Austen keeping her tongue firmly in her cheek when using a traditional aspect of comedy, and leaving us with a final joke at the expense of Mr Woodhouse.

To avoid sentimentality, Jane Austen does not fill her final pages with eye-witness details of the marriage of Mr Knightley and Emma; on the contrary, it is reported to us at third hand by Mrs Elton of all people! 'Very little white satin, very few lace veils; a most pitiful business!' is her summing up of the proceedings, described to her by her husband. Jane Austen has the confidence in us to know that we see through such a character by now, and thus the irony is not lost on us.

Jane Austen has shown herself sympathetic to the great tradition of literary comedy, but she has adapted and developed its features for her own particular uses in her own very special ways. It is a notable feature of this novel that it can be understood within the tradition of comedy, and yet the novel is not constrained within that tradition, for *Emma* has added to it, and has itself become a landmark within that tradition.

AFTERTHOUGHTS

1

What do you understand to be the difference between a caricature and a character?

2

What do you see to be the relationship between humour and irony?

3

Show how Turner's detailed analysis of the portrait-painting in chapter 6 (pages 100–102) relates to this essay as a whole.

4

What do you understand by Turner's distinction between 'true' and 'sentimental' comedy (page 102)?

Peter Hollindale

Peter Hollindale is Senior Lecturer in English and Education at the University of York. He is General Editor of the Macmillan Shakespeare, and has produced numerous books and articles.

ESSAY

Age and patronage in *Emma*

Emma Woodhouse, we are told in the first sentence of the novel, 'had lived nearly twenty-one years in the world with very little to distress or vex her'. Not for nothing do we know the heroine's precise age from the outset. It is the first of many references to people's ages, concentrated mainly though not exclusively in the early chapters. This may seem obvious and unsurprising. We are accustomed to knowing the ages of fictional characters, just as we expect to be told the ages of people mentioned in newspaper reports. Often these are not very important: even in fiction there are many situations where a difference of ten or twenty years in a character's reported age has very little effect on his or her relationships with others. In this novel, however, ages *are* important. They form an intricate pattern which deeply influences the heroine's development. There is not a single major character whose age does not affect Emma's progression from eccentric happiness at the beginning of the novel to natural happiness at the end.

In many cases we know a character's specific age. Before the end of the first chapter we are introduced to Mr Knightley as 'a sensible man about seven or eight-and-thirty', and he himself has told us that Mr Elton ('a very pretty young man', in Mr Woodhouse's helpful phrase) is 'six or seven-and-twenty'. When Emma's plans for future matchmaking begin to evolve, we soon know that Harriet Smith is seventeen and that her would-be husband, Robert Martin, is four-and-twenty. '*Only* four-and-twenty', according to Emma, which seems to her 'too young to settle', a problem of inconvenient youthfulness which Mr Elton at six-and-twenty has presumably overcome. Indeed, later in the novel such youth is by no means an insuperable obstacle for Frank Churchill, who is only twenty-three. Whatever the differences, it is clear from an early stage in the novel that amongst these various bachelors Mr Knightley is distinctly elderly, and the point is underlined by the early revelation that his younger brother, John Knightley, has been married to Emma's sister, Isabella, for long enough to produce a sizeable and growing family. Isabella herself is another whose precise age we know: she is seven years older than Emma. The fact of this long-standing marriage introduces the idea of union between the Woodhouse and Knightley families but also directs our attention to the disparity of age and complicated relationship between the unmarried elder brother of one and younger sister of the other. In every case the exact age matters, or will come to matter in the course of the novel. All but one, we should notice, are older than Emma herself. There is one further character, a belated entrant in the novel, who is exactly the same age as the heroine. This is Jane Fairfax, and she will matter too.

Even in cases where the exact age is not specified, the relationships are meticulously drawn and the omissions presumably deliberate. Jane Austen knows when to be precise, and when to be imprecise. She is imprecise chiefly in two cases: Mr Woodhouse's and Mrs Weston's. Concerning Mr Woodhouse, and his relationship with his daughter, the author presents an early verdict in which kindness and harshness are mixed. It is an important little passage, and serves notice at the start that age, true age, must be computed by something more than the number of birthdays passed:

> The evil of the actual disparity in their ages (and Mr Woodhouse had not married early) was much increased by his constitution and habits; for having been a valetudinarian all his life, without activity of mind or body, he was a much older man in ways than in years; and though everywhere beloved for the friendliness of his heart and his amiable temper, his talents could not have recommended him at any time.
>
> (chapter 1)

Age in Jane Austen is important, but it is modified by attitudes, habits, intelligence and energy. Serious imperfections in these respects, or a failure of balance and harmony between them, are potentially damaging and can produce a human performance which is out of keeping with the individual's actual age in years. In a character (or caricature) such as Mr Woodhouse, the imperfections are permanent and incurable, and the amiable pathos of his behaviour is a lasting reminder of them. But similar discords in the harmony of age and character can occur in far more important and formidable figures, above all in Emma herself. One way of looking at the novel is to see it as presenting the long and often painful process by which Emma's calendar age and her true age — her mind, temperament, feelings and understanding — are brought to a condition of stability and balance. Mr Woodhouse's exact age in years is irrelevant: he will alter only to decline. But Emma, who is twenty-one, is quite different: her calender age conceals inconsistencies of maturity and is a starting point for change. She is not the only character in the novel (though by far the most important one) of whom this is true.

Mr Woodhouse is a negative influence on Emma's life. His premature agedness and mental ineptitude mean not only that he cannot offer her the domestic intellectual stimulus she needs, but that she lacks an observant and responsible father who is alert to her faults and can offer parental guidance. Instead the reverse has happened. Clearly it is Emma who exercises authority at Hartfield, Emma who takes responsibility for Mr Woodhouse's welfare rather than he for hers. In her dealings with him she is impeccably gentle, patient and imaginatively kind; she foresees the serious and the trivial things which will distress him, and averts them. It is a major strength in her. When her efforts at patronage go astray elsewhere, one reason why she never forfeits our sympathy is the knowledge that in her family life she is no stranger to incongruous responsibility. She has to exercise a kind of intimate patronage towards her father, and towards others on his behalf, and she does it conspicuously well. A side-effect of her father's deficiencies is to give to Emma a precocious independence and authority. We cannot blame her too much if she forms a mistaken taste for self-gratifying benevolence. Its roots are in a strange domestic situation which she did not cause and which in itself she handles skilfully.

Until her marriage, Mrs Weston has been the other major figure in Emma's domestic life. We do not know her age, either. She was at Hartfield for sixteen years, and is young enough to bear a child, so we assume that she is somewhere in her late thirties. The vagueness is again important, because it covers her ambiguous role in Emma's life. She is almost old enough to be Emma's mother, a role which she clearly had to supply for a time. But she is almost young enough to be Emma's sister, and for the seven years since Isabella's marriage it is clearly this role which has taken over from substitute maternity. Mrs Weston is presented in the novel as principled, intelligent and charming, and Emma has evidently learned whatever she could from the continuous presence of a good example: we cannot often fault Emma on general grounds of principle, intelligence or charm. What Emma lacks are humility, experience and sound judgement, the qualities that might have developed faster with a bit more maternal discipline and rather less sisterly indulgence. Mrs Weston has done a fair job but not an excellent one as Emma's governess, and the reason again is one of age, with its inevitable consequences for the meeting of mind and attitudes. By age and abilities, Mrs Weston was ambiguously placed towards Emma, and the result has been damaging. Mr Knightley does not mince his words to Mrs Weston in their discussion of Emma. As he sees it, Emma has been spoilt:

> Emma is spoiled by being the cleverest of her family. At ten years old, she had the misfortune of being able to answer questions which puzzled her sister at seventeen. She was always quick and assured: Isabella slow and diffident. And ever since she was twelve, Emma has been mistress of the house and of you all. In her mother she lost the only person able to cope with her.
>
> (chapter 5)

Mr Knightley has been the third major presence in Emma's later childhood, and like her relationships with her father and Miss Taylor this one has been ambiguous and unusual. His interest in Emma's development is justified on social grounds (the Knightleys and the Woodhouses are 'first in consequence' in the neighbourhood of Highbury) and on family grounds (they are linked by the marriage of Mr and Mrs John Knightley, and have exactly the same relationship to the married couple and their children). The difference in their ages, and the origins of their relationship in Emma's early girlhood, have given Mr Knightley an informal role of paternal guardianship which no one else could supply. It has gradually hardened into habit, so that he is accustomed to exercising on Emma the kind of admonishing candour which no one else dares to voice. It extends from very small things ('You have made her too tall, Emma,' he tersely remarks about her portrait of Harriet, in contrast to Mr Elton's lavish praise) to very important ones, such as their quarrel about Harriet's refusal of Robert Martin, and his reproof of Emma's cruelty to Miss Bates.

The relationship strikes us quite early as a little strange. On the one hand, his criticisms are always patently just and necessary. On the other hand they are roughly phrased, and we wonder why Emma, who is no longer a precocious adolescent but twenty-one and proud, should tolerate them as she does. She responds to Mr Knightley's strictures with a curious mixture of the pupil and the equal — with contrition or with spirited self-defence, but scarcely ever with resentment. This is a sign of the relationship's ambiguities: it seems very fixed, but is actually mobile and uncertain. There is something in Mr Knightley left over from the earlier unofficial father, and his own understanding seems stuck with that. But there is also something of the elder brother. And there is something too of the family equal: to the children of the London Knightleys, he is their uncle and Emma is their aunt, and small hints make it clear that in these roles both are attentive, vigorous and popular. We are inclined to wonder whether the respective roles of bachelor uncle and maiden aunt will always meet their needs. The sum of these roles is to make us feel that there is more to this apparently simple relationship than meets the eye. The strength of Mr Knightley's guardian-like interest, and the self-willed Emma's tolerance of it, become steadily more intriguing as the novel proceeds and we get to know them better. Once again ages are the key to unusual and complex friendships. The problem surfaces explicitly in a key passage which repays close attention. It occurs in chapter 12; Knightley is speaking to Emma:

'If you were as much guided by nature in your estimate of men and women, and as little under the power of fancy and whim in your dealings with them, as you are where these children are concerned, we might always think alike.'

'To be sure — our discordancies must always arise from my being in the wrong.'

'Yes,' said he, smiling — 'and reason good. I was sixteen years old when you were born.'

'A material difference, then,' she replied — 'and no doubt you were much my superior in judgement at that period of our lives; but does not the lapse of one-and-twenty years bring our understandings a good deal nearer?'

'Yes — a good deal *nearer*.'

'But still not near enough to give me a chance of being right, if we think differently.'

'I still have the advantage of you by sixteen years' experience, and by not being a pretty young woman and a spoiled child. Come, my dear Emma, let us be friends and say no more about it.'

(chapter 12)

Much of the ambiguity is concentrated expressly in this passage, above all perhaps in the description 'a pretty young woman and a spoiled child'. In that phrase is summarised much that they have still so painfully to discover about each other. For Knightley it hints at the transition of his interest from the child to the woman, although he is still unaware of it himself. (It requires the arrival of twenty-three-year-old Frank Churchill to wake him up.) For Emma the provocative condescension of one phrase is made tolerable by the appealing compliment of the other. We also notice that their disagreement about adults is balanced by mutual respect in their dealings with children. But the most important point about the passage is surely that Emma is right. As they grow older, the difference in experience which is linked to their difference in age will lessen. Knightley will always be sixteen years older in chronological age, but in experience and understanding the space between them will progressively diminish. At the heart of *Emma* is the accelerated closing of that gap. The process of their growing together is speeded up by apparent separation — by misunderstandings, false suppositions, error and jealously on *both* sides, and by a severe ordeal of emotional pain.

Because the novel is chiefly about Emma, it is her consciousness through which we experience the pain most vividly. But that should not cause us to overlook the balancing development of Knightley. We can simplify a complex process in this way. It is easy to see that through bitter experience Emma grows older. What is less obvious is that Mr Knightley grows younger. For him the inadvertent catalyst of new feelings is the young Frank Churchill, and the disconcerting jealousy he rouses. Mr Knightley is not a fixed point, a static figure of whom Emma gradually becomes worthy. He changes too. And he is not so dignified a figure that Jane Austen can have no fun at his expense. At the end of chapter 49, after his triumphant sudden courtship, she enjoys depicting him as the youthful lover, with the youthful lover's comic instability of judgement:

> He had found her agitated and low. — Frank Churchill was a villain. — He heard her declare that she had never loved him. Frank Churchill's character was not desperate. — She was his own Emma, by hand and word, when they returned into the house; and if he could have thought of Frank Churchill then, he might have deemed him a very good sort of fellow.'

(chapter 49)

A little later, in chapter 52, Mr Knightley's belated plunge into romantic youthfulness is comically testified by Mr Elton, who has endured a hot walk to Donwell Abbey to meet him. Knightley has uncharacteristically forgotten the arrangement and wandered off, 'Perhaps to Hartfield, perhaps to the Abbey Mill, perhaps into the woods'.

What happens to both Emma and Mr Knightley, in fact, is the collapse of a precarious self-sufficiency. For the immediate trials and final happiness of this process, the two of them owe some curious debts. I have tried to demonstrate that Emma's character, its curious mixture of virtues and weaknesses, can be largely explained by accidents of age and oddities of circumstance in the limited circle of people who affect her growing-up at Hartfield. The normal relationships are missing, and the ones that replaced them are ambiguous. By inference, much the same is true of Mr Knightley. If his bachelorhood has been protracted, we cannot see any eligible person in the neighbourhood of Highbury who might previously have lured him from it. Now that Emma is a woman, it is easy for his feelings to change towards her, but much less easy for him to realise that they have. Habit dies hard. Two novelties which seem to threaten their existing relationship actually help it to grow and develop. One is the arrival in Highbury of several people who form the 'missing' age-group of young adults, represented hitherto only by Emma herself: first Mr Elton, joined in due course by his appalling wife, and later Jane Fairfax and Frank Churchill. The misunderstandings generated in various ways by this quarter allow the pattern to change. The second important novelty is Harriet.

Harriet, we noted earlier, is the only important character who is *younger* than Emma herself. It is one of the novel's neatest ironies that two acts of patronage towards Harriet lead to Emma's most crucial self-discoveries. In the early part of the novel it is Emma who adopts the role of patron. She will do good to Harriet; she will improve her; she will marry her off to Mr Elton. The first of Emma's mortifying discoveries about herself is that both the Knightley brothers have been right about Mr Elton and she has been wrong. In the later stages of the novel, Harriet's patron is Mr Knightley. His patronage, which generates so much misunderstanding, begins with his act of kindness at the ball. Pleasantly surprised to find that Harriet is less stupid than he thought (and hence that Emma was not *wholly* wrong!) he undertakes a patronage of his own towards her. Its purpose (as Emma's initial patronage was supposed to be) is altruistic. He wishes to correct Emma's original error and restore Harriet to Robert Martin. Unlike Emma, he is quiet and discreet about it. But just like Emma, he is not immune from other people's misconceptions. Emma's purposes were misinterpreted by Mr Elton; Mr Knightley's are misunderstood by Harriet herself. And Harriet's version of events is plausible enough to frighten Emma into her second major self-discovery: the realisation of her true feelings.

The idea of patronage is a useful one in understanding *Emma*, but is must be treated with some care. Jane Austen is describing a society where social positions and gradations are fixed and important, and often separated by delicate nuances of status. (Consider Emma's debate in chapter 25 — as to whether she can dine with the Coles.) In such a society, patronage is an essential part of the social order. Emma states the position baldly when she is busily turning Harriet against Robert Martin:

> The yeomanry are precisely the order of people with whom I feel I can have nothing to do. A degree or two lower, and a creditable appearance might interest me; I might hope to be useful to their families in some way or other. But a farmer can need none of my help, and is therefore is one sense as much above my notice as in every other he is below it.'

(chapter 4)

However, in a society which has such differences of wealth, together with such intimacy of personal knowledge and acquaintance, patronage is not just a matter of snobbery, or social status, or even of riches. It extents to many acts of benevolence and thoughtfulness by which the well-placed care for others. A very thin line separates patronage defined by public status and social charity from patronage expressed through sympathetic personal relationships. We need to bring to it (as Austen's intelligent characters themselves do) a moral judgement rather than a social judgement. On this criterion Mr Knightley's acts of patronage are admirably discreet, thoughtful and unselfish, whether he is giving his last apples to Miss Bates, dancing with Harriet, assisting Robert Martin, or behaving tactfully to Mr Woodhouse. At the opposite extreme are Mrs Elton's vulgar and insensitive attentions to Jane Fairfax. These are a much cruder and coarser version of Emma's patronage of Harriet, but the resemblance is there for us to see. Both are too much concerned with self-gratification and too little with generous and unbigoted human judgement.

The same self-interested motive accounts for Emma's neglect and dislike of Jane Fairfax. Jane is elegant and accomplished, an appropriate and equal companion for Emma in all but means. For Emma to show her attention would be *legitimate* patronage, a selfless expression of respect. But by the time she has learned to judge Jane fairly, patronage is no longer called for. What Knightley knows, Emma finds out, and Mrs Elton could never learn, is that true patronage is not the same at all as being patronising. It is a difficult distinction for modern readers to make, but we cannot fully understand *Emma* without it.

In their gradual meeting of ages, and abandonment on both sides of their illusory self-sufficiency, we can see Emma and Knightley growing towards each other; and in the displacement of Emma's patronage of Harriet by Knightley's, we can see the mature standards of judgement and sensitivity which they have finally come to share. It is the novel's subtle exploration of age and of patronage which gives conviction to the happy ending. Emma and Knightley will always be sixteen years apart, but in all the ways that matter they end the novel as equals.

AFTERTHOUGHTS

1

What relationship is established in this essay between age and patronage?

2

What significance does Hollindale see in the fact that neither Mr Woodhouse nor Mrs Weston is given a precise age? Do you agree?

3

Do you agree with Hollindale's argument that both Emma *and* Mr Knightley have changed by the end of the novel?

4

What distinction is drawn in this essay between 'true patronage' and 'being patronising' (page 113)?

Cedric Watts

Cedric Watts is Professor of English at Sussex University, and author of numerous scholarly publications.

ESSAY

The limitations of *Emma*

From students and fellow-teachers I still, sometimes, hear this kind of comment on Jane Austen: 'She's an intelligently ironic and subtle writer, but of course she has her limitations. Her novels don't deal with battles or turbulent passions or far-off regions. Everything's on a small scale. She wrote about what she knew; and, as a clergyman's daughter living in the rural south and west of England, she knew best the quiet lives of the gentry in the shires.' It's a rather patronising comment. 'She wrote about what she knew'; and the implication is that she didn't know very much. What such comments fail to register is that, to a large extent, Jane Austen's 'limitations' are aggressive challenges.

Dates are instructive. Jane Austen was born in 1775 and died in 1817: *Emma* was published in 1816. That novel appeared, then, in the heyday of the English romantic movement — the time of celebration of passionate intensities. Wordsworth and Coleridge were growing in reputation; Byron, Shelley and Keats were publishing important poems; and the 'Gothic' novel was very popular. The action of a Gothic novel is usually set in the past, in late medieval or Renaissance times rather than the present. The location is usually non-English: it might be Spain or Italy or France. And such novels provided supernatural (or apparently supernatural) terrors, haunted castles or abbeys, gloomy dungeons, grisly horrors, melodramatic events, villains who were very villainous and heroes or heroines who were heroically virtuous. The beautiful, virtuous and gifted heroine of Mrs Radcliffe's *The Mysteries of Udolpho* travels through France, Italy and the Pyrenees, is abducted and held prisoner, is subjected to appalling dangers and fears, but preserves herself immaculate for marriage to a reformed adventurer. In M G Lewis's *The Monk*, the central figure is the wicked monk, Ambrosio, a murderous rapist who sells his soul to the devil; eventually the devil himself carries Ambrosio high into the air and lets him fall to his death on a rocky peak of the mountain range. Jane Austen knew such works well and was keenly critical of them.

In Austen's *Northanger Abbey*, the heroine is an impressionable young Englishwoman who, having read uncritically a large number of Gothic novels, persuades herself that Northanger Abbey itself, where she is a guest, may hold some hideous secret, and that her host, General Tilney, may have emulated the evil Montoni in *The Mysteries of Udolpho* by killing his wife. Eventually the general's son learns of the guest's delusions; and this is his reproach:

> 'Dear Miss Morland, consider the dreadful nature of the suspicions you have entertained. What have you been judging from? Remember the country and the age in which we live. Remember that we are English, that we are Christians. Consult your own understanding, your own sense of the probable, your own observation of what is passing around you. . . . Dearest Miss Morland, what ideas have you been admitting?'
>
> They had reached the end of the gallery; and with tears of shame she ran off to her own room.
>
> (*Northanger Abbey*, chapter 24)

Jane Austen is directing those words not only to Miss Morland but also to the reader. 'Consult your own understanding, your own sense of the probable.' Explicitly in *Northanger Abbey*, implicitly throughout her novels, and most brilliantly in *Emma*, she is the champion of plausible realism and the foe of romantic excess and Gothic extravagance. The Gothic novels melodramatised the past; *Emma* concentrates on the present. A Gothic heroine might hasten through Europe; Emma is familiar with a small part of provincial England. And instead of the blatant appeals of romanticism to the emotions, Jane Austen's intricate use of irony obliges the reader to work with cool intelligence on the text, reading between the lines, collaborating with a shrewdly watchful author. The plots of Gothic novels are frequently entangled, digressive, repetitive and disjointed; her plotting of *Emma* is concise, systematic and adroit: nothing is superfluous. Thus, many of the apparent limitations of Jane Austen prove to be a deliberate challenge to a predominantly romantic literary culture. She writes of the familiar world and not of the exotic world. She writes of people for whom violence and aggression are not matters of bullets or rapiers or poisoned goblets, but rather matters of a snobbish remark or thoughtless gesture. She writes to the constraints imposed not by dungeons, fetters and satanic pacts but by class, income and gender. Her novels of education serve to educate the reader in the significance of the commonplace. Today we tend to take realism for granted, because there's so much of it about: it provides the central tradition in novels, films, TV plays. But there was a time when realism had to be fought for; and Jane Austen was one of the great fighters, a forerunner of Elizabeth Gaskell, George Eliot and Thomas Hardy. In her time, Austen was extraordinary in her fidelity to the ordinary, and profound in her depiction of the mundane. A fellow-novelist of her day, Sir Walter Scott, understood the challenge, saying of her work:

> [A] style of novel has arisen . . . differing from the former in the points upon which the interest hinges; neither alarming our credulity nor amusing our imagination by wild variety of incident, or by those pictures of romantic affection and sensibility, which were formerly as certain attributes of fictitious characters as they are of rare occurrence among those who actually live and die. The substitute for these excitements, which had lost much of their poignancy by the repeated and injudicious use of them, [is] the art of copying from nature as she really exists in the common walks of life, and presenting to the reader, instead of the splendid scenes of an imaginary world, a correct and striking representation of what is daily taking place in the world around him.[1]

---

[1] Essay in *Quarterly Review*, March 1816, quoted in David Lodge (ed.), *Jane Austen: 'Emma'* (Macmillan Casebook; London, 1968), p.39.

The realities of class, income, gender, education: all these received a new, detailed accuracy of attention in her novels; and the main coordination is provided by her concern with selfishness and unselfishness. If you see a film or television serial or video of *Emma*, you'll find that the camera inevitably makes visual matters much more prominent than they were in the novel: we notice the Regency costumes, the rumbling coaches, the charming old houses. The novel, on the other hand, repeatedly makes surfaces transparent, for we're obliged to look beneath appearances to the moral natures of the characters. Indeed, the text (in its multiple ironies) offers a training in resistance to obvious appearances. Some authors make realism seem a matter of plodding reportage; but Jane Austen saw that since subjectivity — and particularly selfishness — are constantly distorting and falsifying our understanding of the world, a realistic text can quite properly offer multiple overlapping narratives. Different characters interpret information in different ways; and we, as readers, are soon involved in the quest to distinguish truth from false inference. For much of the time in *Emma*, we see through the eyes, or at least over the shoulder, of a heroine whose egotism distorts her perceptions; and the result is a lively double-plot. There's the overt plot: the events as Emma perceives them. There's also the covert plot: the real events which are often in ironic contrast to her perception of them. Not until the ending of the novel, when all is made plain to Emma, does the covert plot finally surface and become identical with the overt plot. So the reader of the text constantly has to construct the true sequence, making allowance for the distortions created by snobbery and egotism. That's what gives Jane Austen's work its staying-power: the pleasure of the text is a strenuous pleasure because we gain a complicated insight into the distortions generated by subjectivity. As long as selfishness remains, as long as subjectivity leads to false readings of the world, her work will remain relevant. She tells stories about the ways in which we all make stories of life; and she argues that the more selfish we are, the less realistic those stories will be. *Emma* is a subtle comedy of false perceptions; but at the same time it's an intense moral analysis of the difficulty of seeing clearly and understanding truly. She makes the readers collaborators in the analysis; she writes moral and psychological detective stories. And her ironies are so densely layered that for most readers it may be only at the second or even at the third reading of *Emma* that their full extent can be seen. In its implications, this is a much bigger and deeper text than first appears; and one of those implications is that readers who see it as a rather limited work may be imposing upon it their own limited intelligence. The reader may sometimes be ambushed by its ironies.

But sometimes even Jane Austen may be ambushed by them. Consider her treatment of snobbery, for example. When Emma persuades Harriet Smith to reject Robert Martin, her snobbery is blatant, and she will later be abundantly punished for it. Advising Harriet to decline the proposal of marriage, made in a fine letter 'which would not have disgraced a gentleman', Emma says:

> You would have thrown yourself out of all good society. I must have given you up. . . . *You* banished to Abbey-Mill Farm! *You* confined to the society of the illiterate and vulgar all your life! I wonder how the young man could have the assurance to ask it.

(chapter 7)

Harriet is persuaded; Martin is rejected; and the injustice of Emma's view of Martin is repeatedly emphasised. His letter was impressive even to Emma; Mr Knightley angrily rebukes Emma for thinking that it could be 'a degradation' for the illegitimate Harriet to marry a man esteemed as 'a respectable, intelligent gentleman-farmer'. And the plot proceeds to heap ample ironic punishment on Emma. Thinking that she is successfully manipulating Harriet into marriage to Mr Elton, Emma is shocked and humiliated to find herself the object of a proposal from Elton, who had misconstrued her wiles. Next, Emma believes that she is successfully arranging for Harriet to fall in love with Frank Churchill, and is indignant to discover that Harriet has in fact been attracted to Mr Knightley (which leads Emma to discover her own love for Knightley). And eventually, largely through Knightley's quiet diplomacy, Harriet marries Robert Martin after all. So snobbery seems to be amply punished. Yet, when the impending marriage of Harriet to Martin is being discussed, this is what the wise and observant Mr Knightley says to Emma about him:

> His situation is an evil. . . . As far as the man is concerned, you
> could not wish your friend in better hands. His rank in society
> I would alter if I could . . .
>
> (chapter 54)

And this is how Harriet's parentage is described:

> Harriet's parentage became known. She proved to be the
> daughter of a tradesman, rich enough to afford her the comfort-
> able maintenance which had ever been hers, and decent enough
> to have always wished for concealment. — Such was the blood
> of gentility which Emma had formerly been so ready to vouch
> for! — It was likely to be as untainted, perhaps, as the blood of
> many a gentleman: but what a connexion had she been
> preparing for Mr Knightley — or for the Churchills — or even
> for Mr Elton! — The stain of illegitimacy, unbleached by
> nobility or wealth, would have been a stain indeed.
>
> (chapter 55)

So, in the eyes of their social superiors, Mr Martin, gentleman-
farmer, is in an 'evil' situation, in an undesirable rank; while
Harriet Smith is indeed 'stained' by an illegitimacy (not of her
choosing), for it is 'unbleached' by nobility or wealth. When I
said that Jane Austen is sometimes ambushed by her own
ironies, I meant that they may invoke moral standards that the
text eventually seems to betray. When we see the injustice of
Emma's initial snobbish response to Martin, we infer the moral
recommendation that the worth of individuals should be
assessed on the basis of their merits of character and not by
their social rank or their circumstances of birth. But the final
assessments, in the text, of Martin and Harriet Smith make
bigger compromises with prejudice than we wish. Jane Austen
might retort: 'That's my realism. These are the judgements that
decent people in my day actually make. Don't be sentimental;
don't be anachronistic. In my lifetime the French Revolution has
resulted in dictatorship and mass slaughter, so don't expect me
to propose revolutionary social change.' Yet it is her own
narrative, her own critique of snobbery, that has created our
misgivings.

Again, consider the plight of Jane Fairfax. She is superior

in abilities to Emma, but she lacks Emma's large unearned income; so, unless the procrastinating Frank Churchill can make good his promise to marry her, she faces a future in the governess-trade — via 'Offices for the sale — not quite of human flesh — but of human intellect' (chapter 35). Her plight emphasises the fact that individuals of talent and sensitivity may be forced into humble social strata, just as the instance of Mrs Elton shows that people of wealth and station may be insufferably vulgar. If *Emma* ends as comedy, it does so because, for the characters with whom we sympathise, the possibility of tragedy has been averted: the ingenuous Harriet marries Martin after all; and the sensitive Jane Fairfax is redeemed by marriage from the governess-trade. Yet the possibility of tragedy, though averted, has been raised; and consequently the novel has raised larger questions about social injustice than it answers. It is a limitation in Jane Austen's fiction that we see so little of the servants, the waiters at the rich people's tables, the humble cottagers so charitably visited by Emma; but it is the socially probing ironies of Jane Austen which make us aware of those limitations. Here criticism of the text is tied to praise. In the famous instance of Knightley's rebuke to Emma for her rudeness to Miss Bates, the text itself makes us aware of the claims of the humble and impoverished; it tells us that egotism makes us socially short-sighted. Yet that in turn makes us more conscious than we would otherwise be of a kind of short-sightedness in Jane Austen's social range. No author can describe everything; every author has to select. But when a text has repeatedly, through its ironies, offered warnings against an egoistic blindness to the just claims and needs of others, its own selectivities in characterisation become conspicuous and problematic.

Jane Austen writes with immense lucidity, shrewdness and economy. She offers a finely rational account of a world in which human conduct is subject to rationally explicable laws. But, descriptively, in her treatment of the world available to the senses, the texture of her prose is thin: we don't gain a strong impression of the smells of food, the feel of bodies, the sweat of dancers. If she placed more emphasis on the sensuous, she might be placing more emphasis on forces that subvert the rational judgement; her world would then be more turbulent, less placid, less controllable. The relationship between Emma and Mr Knightley may eventually seem to resemble that between a wayward but intelligent pupil and a patient teacher, rather than a relationship of lovers heading for a honeymoon. For bedside reading, perhaps they need a few romantic poems — or even a Gothic novel.

AFTERTHOUGHTS

1

'She wrote about what she knew' (page 116). Can one ever write about anything else?

2

What distinction does Watts draw between 'overt plot' and 'covert plot' (page 119)?

3

What do you understand by Watts's comment that Jane Austen is 'sometimes ambushed by her own ironies'? What examples does he give?

4

Compare this essay with Pinsent's approach to a similar question (pages 9–19). How does the focus differ?

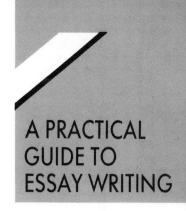

A PRACTICAL GUIDE TO ESSAY WRITING

INTRODUCTION

First, a word of warning. Good essays are the product of a creative engagement with literature. So never try to restrict your studies to what you think will be 'useful in the exam'. Ironically, you will restrict your grade potential if you do.

This doesn't mean, of course, that you should ignore the basic skills of essay writing. When you read critics, make a conscious effort to notice *how* they communicate their ideas. The guidelines that follow offer advice of a more explicit kind. But they are no substitute for practical experience. It is never easy to express ideas with clarity and precision. But the more often you tackle the problems involved and experiment to find your own voice, the more fluent you will become. So practise writing essays as often as possible.

HOW TO PLAN
AN ESSAY

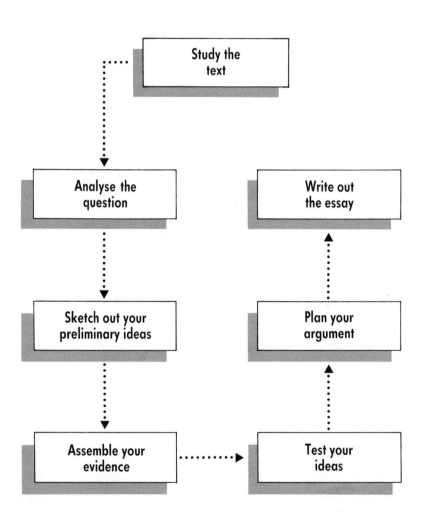

Study the
text

Analyse the
question

Write out
the essay

Sketch out your
preliminary ideas

Plan your
argument

Assemble your
evidence

Test your
ideas

Study the text

The first step in writing a good essay is to get to know the set text well. Never write about a text until you are fully familiar with it. Even a discussion of the opening chapter of a novel, for example, should be informed by an understanding of the book as a whole. Literary texts, however, are by their very nature complex and on a first reading you are bound to miss many significant features. Re-read the book with care, if possible more than once. Look up any unfamiliar words in a good dictionary and if the text you are studying was written more than a few decades ago, consult the *Oxford English Dictionary* to find out whether the meanings of any terms have shifted in the intervening period.

Good books are difficult to put down when you first read them. But a more leisurely second or third reading gives you the opportunity to make notes on those features you find significant. An index of characters and events is often useful, particularly when studying novels with a complex plot or time scheme. The main aim, however, should be to record your *responses* to the text. By all means note, for example, striking images. But be sure to add *why* you think them striking. Similarly, record any thoughts you may have on interesting comparisons with other texts, puzzling points of characterisation, even what you take to be aesthetic blemishes. The important thing is to annotate fully and adventurously. The most seemingly idiosyncratic comment may later lead to a crucial area of discussion which you would otherwise have overlooked. It helps to have a working copy of the text in which to mark up key passages and jot down marginal comments (although obviously these practices are taboo when working with library, borrowed or valuable copies!). But keep a fuller set of notes as well and organise these under appropriate headings.

Literature does not exist in an aesthetic vacuum, however, and you should try to find out as much as possible about the context of its production and reception. It is particularly important to read other works by the same author and writings by contemporaries. At this early stage, you may want to restrict your secondary reading to those standard reference works, such as biographies, which are widely available in public libraries. In the long run, however, it pays to read as wide a range of critical studies as possible.

Some students, and tutors, worry that such studies may stifle the development of any truly personal response. But this won't happen if you are alert to the danger and read critically. After all, you wouldn't passively accept what a stranger told you in conversation. The fact that a critic's views are in print does not necessarily make them any more authoritative (as a glance at the review pages of the *TLS* and *London Review of Books* will reveal). So question the views you find: 'Does this critic's interpretation agree with mine and where do we part company?' 'Can it be right to try and restrict this text's meanings to those found by its author or first audience?' 'Doesn't this passage treat a theatrical text as though it were a novel?' Often it is views which you reject which prove most valuable since they challenge you to articulate your own position with greater clarity. Be sure to keep careful notes on what the critic wrote, and your *reactions* to what the critic wrote.

Analyse the question

You cannot begin to answer a question until you understand what task it is you have been asked to perform. Recast the question in your own words and reconstruct the line of reasoning which lies behind it. Where there is a choice of topics, try to choose the one for which you are best prepared. It would, for example, be unwise to tackle 'How far do you agree that in *Paradise Lost* Milton transformed the epic models he inherited from ancient Greece and Rome?' without a working knowledge of Homer and Virgil (or *Paradise Lost* for that matter!). If you do not already know the works of these authors, the question should spur you on to read more widely — or discourage you from attempting it at all. The scope of an essay, however, is not always so obvious and you must remain alert to the implied demands of each question. How could you possibly 'Consider the view that *Wuthering Heights* transcends the conventions of the Gothic novel' without reference to at least some of those works which, the question suggests, have *not* transcended Gothic conventions?

When you have decided on a topic, analyse the terms of the question itself. Sometimes these self-evidently require careful definition: *tragedy* and *irony*, for example, are notoriously difficult concepts to pin down and you will probably need to consult a good dictionary of literary terms. Don't ignore, however, those seemingly innocuous phrases which often smuggle in significant assumptions. 'Does Macbeth lack the nobility of the true tragic hero?' obviously invites you to discuss nobility and the nature of the tragic hero. But what of 'lack' and 'true' — do they suggest that the play would be improved had Shakespeare depicted Macbeth in a different manner? or that tragedy is superior to other forms of drama? Remember that you are not expected meekly to agree with the assumptions implicit in the question. Some questions are deliberately provocative in order to stimulate an engaged response. Don't be afraid to take up the challenge.

Sketch out your preliminary ideas

'Which comes first, the evidence or the answer?' is one of those chicken and egg questions. How can you form a view without inspecting the evidence? But how can you know which evidence is relevant without some idea of what it is you are looking for? In practice the mind reviews evidence and formulates preliminary theories or hypotheses at one and the same time, although for the sake of clarity we have separated out the processes. Remember that these early ideas are only there to get you started. You *expect* to modify them in the light of the evidence you uncover. Your initial hypothesis may be an instinctive 'gut-reaction'. Or you may find that you prefer to 'sleep on the problem', allowing ideas to gell over a period of time. Don't worry in either case. The mind is quite capable of processing a vast amount of accumulated evidence, the product of previous reading and thought, and reaching sophisticated intuitive judgements. Eventually, however, you are going to have to think carefully through any ideas you arrive at by such intuitive processes. Are they logical? Do they take account of all the relevant factors? Do they fully answer the question set? Are there any obvious reasons to qualify or abandon them?

Assemble your evidence

Now is the time to return to the text and re-read it with the question and your working hypothesis firmly in mind. Many of the notes you have already made are likely to be useful, but assess the precise relevance of this material and make notes on any new evidence you discover. The important thing is to cast your net widely and take into account points which tend to undermine your case as well as those that support it. As always, ensure that your notes are full, accurate, and reflect your own critical judgements.

You may well need to go outside the text if you are to do full justice to the question. If you think that the 'Oedipus complex' may be relevant to an answer on *Hamlet* then read Freud and a balanced selection of those critics who have discussed the appropriateness of applying psychoanalytical theories to the interpretation of literature. Their views can most easily be tracked down by consulting the annotated bibliographies held by most major libraries (and don't be afraid to ask a librarian for help in finding and using these). Remember that you go to works of criticism not only to obtain information but to stimulate you into clarifying your own position. And that since life is short and many critical studies are long, judicious use of a book's index and/or contents list is not to be scorned. You can save yourself a great deal of future labour if you carefully record full bibliographic details at this stage.

Once you have collected the evidence, organise it coherently. Sort the detailed points into related groups and identify the quotations which support these. You must also assess the relative importance of each point, for in an essay of limited length it is essential to establish a firm set of priorities, exploring some ideas in depth while discarding or subordinating others.

Test your ideas

As we stressed earlier, a hypothesis is only a proposal, and one that you fully expect to modify. Review it with the evidence before you. Do you really still believe in it? It would be surprising if you did not want to modify it in some way. If you cannot see any problems, others may. Try discussing your ideas with friends and relatives. Raise them in class discussions. Your tutor is certain to welcome your initiative. The critical process is essentially collaborative and there is absolutely no reason why you should not listen to and benefit from the views of others. Similarly, you should feel free to test your ideas against the theories put forward in academic journals and books. But do not just borrow what you find. Critically analyse the views on offer and, where appropriate, integrate them into your own pattern of thought. You must, of course, give full acknowledgement to the sources of such views.

Do not despair if you find you have to abandon or modify significantly your initial position. The fact that you are prepared to do so is a mark of intellectual integrity. Dogmatism is never an academic virtue and many of the best essays explore the *process* of scholarly enquiry rather than simply record its results.

Plan your argument

Once you have more or less decided on your attitude to the question (for an answer is never really 'finalised') you have to present your case in the most persuasive manner. In order to do this you must avoid meandering from point to point and instead produce an organised argument — a structured flow of ideas and supporting evidence, leading logically to a conclusion which fully answers the question. Never begin to write until you have produced an outline of your argument.

You may find it easiest to begin by sketching out its main stage as a flow chart or some other form of visual presentation. But eventually you should produce a list of paragraph topics. The paragraph is the conventional written demarcation for a unit of thought and you can outline an argument quite simply by briefly summarising the substance of each paragraph and then checking that these points (you may remember your English teacher referring to them as topic sentences) really do follow a coherent order. Later you will be able to elaborate on each topic, illustrating and qualifying it as you go along. But you will find this far easier to do if you possess from the outset a clear map of where you are heading.

All questions require some form of an argument. Even so-called 'descriptive' questions *imply* the need for an argument. An adequate answer to the request to 'Outline the role of Iago in *Othello*' would do far more than simply list his appearances on stage. It would at the very least attempt to provide some *explanation* for his actions — is he, for example, a representative stage 'Machiavel'? an example of pure evil, 'motiveless malignity'? or a realistic study of a tormented personality reacting to identifiable social and psychological pressures?

Your conclusion ought to address the terms of the question. It may seem obvious, but 'how far do you agree', 'evaluate', 'consider', 'discuss', etc, are *not* interchangeable formulas and your conclusion must take account of the precise wording of the question. If asked 'How far do you agree?', the concluding paragraph of your essay really should state whether you are in complete agreement, total disagreement, or, more likely, partial agreement. Each preceding paragraph should have a clear justification for its existence and help to clarify the reasoning which underlies your conclusion. If you find that a paragraph serves no good purpose (perhaps merely summarising the plot), do not hesitate to discard it.

The arrangement of the paragraphs, the overall strategy of the argument, can vary. One possible pattern is dialectical: present the arguments in favour of one point of view (**thesis**); then turn to counter-arguments or to a rival interpretation (**antithesis**); finally evaluate the competing claims and arrive at your own conclusion (**synthesis**). You may, on the other hand, feel so convinced of the merits of one particular case that you wish to devote your entire essay to arguing that viewpoint persuasively (although it is always desirable to indicate, however briefly, that you are aware of alternative, if flawed, positions). As the essays contained in this volume demonstrate, there are many other possible strategies. Try to adopt the one which will most comfortably accommodate the demands of the question and allow you to express your thoughts with the greatest possible clarity.

Be careful, however, not to apply abstract formulas in a mechanical manner. It is true that you should be careful to define your terms. It is *not* true that every essay should begin with 'The dictionary defines x as . . .'. In fact, definitions are often best left until an appropriate moment for their introduction arrives. Similarly every essay should have a beginning, middle and end. But it does not follow that in your opening paragraph you should announce an intention to write an essay, or that in your concluding paragraph you need to signal an imminent desire to put down your pen. The old adages are often useful reminders of what constitutes good practice, but they must be interpreted intelligently.

Write out the essay

Once you have developed a coherent argument you should aim to communicate it in the most effective manner possible. Make certain you clearly identify yourself, and the question you are answering. Ideally, type your answer, or at least ensure your handwriting is legible and that you leave sufficient space for your tutor's comments. Careless presentation merely distracts from the force of your argument. Errors of grammar, syntax and spelling are far more serious. At best they are an irritating blemish, particularly in the work of a student who should be sensitive to the nuances of language. At worst, they seriously confuse the sense of your argument. If you are aware that you have stylistic problems of this kind, ask your tutor for advice at the earliest opportunity. Everyone, however, is liable to commit the occasional howler. The only remedy is to give yourself plenty of time in which to proof-read your manuscript (often reading it aloud is helpful) before submitting it.

Language, however, is not only an instrument of communication; it is also an instrument of thought. If you want to think clearly and precisely you should strive for a clear, precise prose style. Keep your sentences short and direct. Use modern, straightforward English wherever possible. Avoid repetition, clichés and wordiness. Beware of generalisations, simplifications, and overstatements. Orwell analysed the relationship between stylistic vice and muddled thought in his essay 'Politics and the English Language' (1946) — it remains essential reading (and is still readily available in volume 4 of the Penguin *Collected Essays, Journalism and Letters*). Generalisations, for example, are always dangerous. They are rarely true and tend to suppress the individuality of the texts in question. A remark such as 'Keats always employs sensuous language in his poetry' is not only fatuous (what, after all, does it mean? is *every* word he wrote equally 'sensuous'?) but tends to obscure interesting distinctions which could otherwise be made between, say, the descriptions in the 'Ode on a Grecian Urn' and those in 'To Autumn'.

The intelligent use of quotations can help you make your points with greater clarity. Don't sprinkle them throughout your essay without good reason. There is no need, for example, to use them to support uncontentious statements of fact. 'Macbeth murdered Duncan' does not require textual evidence (unless you wish to dispute Thurber's brilliant parody, 'The Great Macbeth Murder Mystery', which reveals Lady Macbeth's father as the culprit!). Quotations should be included, however, when they are necessary to support your case. The proposition that Macbeth's imaginative powers wither after he has killed his king would certainly require extensive quotation: you would almost certainly want to analyse key passages from both before and after the murder (perhaps his first and last soliloquies?). The key word here is 'analyse'. Quotations cannot make your points on their own. It is up to you to demonstrate their relevance and clearly explain to your readers *why* you want them to focus on the passage you have selected.

Most of the academic conventions which govern the presentation of essays are set out briefly in the style sheet below. The question of gender, however, requires fuller discussion. More than half the population of the world is female. Yet many writers still refer to an undifferentiated *man*kind. Or write of the author and *his* public. We do not think that this convention has much to recommend it. At the very least, it runs the risk of introducing unintended sexist attitudes. And at times leads to such patent absurdities as 'Cleopatra's final speech asserts *man*'s true nobility'. With a little thought, you can normally find ways of expressing yourself which do not suggest that the typical author, critic or reader is male. Often you can simply use plural forms, which is probably a more elegant solution than relying on such awkward formulations as 's/he' or 'he and she'. You should also try to avoid distinguishing between male and female authors on the basis of forenames. Why *Jane* Austen and not *George* Byron? Refer to all authors by their last names unless there is some good reason not to. Where there may otherwise be confusion, say between T S and George Eliot, give the name in full when it first occurs and thereafter use the last name only.

Finally, keep your audience firmly in mind. Tutors and examiners are interested in understanding your conclusions and the processes by which you arrived at them. They are not interested in reading a potted version of a book they already know. **So don't pad out your work with plot summary.**

Hints for examinations

In an examination you should go through exactly the same processes as you would for the preparation of a term essay. The only difference lies in the fact that some of the stages will have had to take place before you enter the examination room. This should not bother you unduly. Examiners are bound to avoid the merely eccentric when they come to formulate papers and if you have read widely and thought deeply about the central issues raised by your set texts you can be confident you will have sufficient material to answer the majority of questions sensibly.

The fact that examinations impose strict time limits makes it *more* rather than less, important that you plan carefully. There really is no point in floundering into an answer without any idea of where you are going, particularly when there will not be time to recover from the initial error.

Before you begin to answer any question at all, study the entire paper with care. Check that you understand the rubric and know how many questions you have to answer and whether any are compulsory. It may be comforting to spot a title you feel confident of answering well, but don't rush to tackle it: read *all* the questions before deciding which *combination* will allow you to display your abilities to the fullest advantage. Once you have made your choice, analyse each question, sketch out your ideas, assemble the evidence, review your initial hypothesis, play your argument, *before* trying to write out an answer. And make notes at each stage: not only will these help you arrive at a sensible conclusion, but examiners are impressed by evidence of careful thought.

Plan your time as well as your answers. If you have practised writing timed essays as part of your revision, you should not find this too difficult. There can be a temptation to allocate extra time to the questions you know you can answer well; but this is always a short-sighted policy. You will find yourself left to face a question which would in any event have given you difficulty without even the time to give it serious thought. It is, moreover, easier to gain marks at the lower end of the scale than at the upper, and you will never compensate for one poor answer by further polishing two satisfactory answers. Try to leave some time at the end of the examination to re-read your answers and correct any obvious errors. If the worst comes to the worst and you run short of time, don't just keep writing until you are forced to break off in mid-paragraph. It is far better to provide for the examiner a set of notes which indicate the overall direction of your argument.

Good luck — but if you prepare for the examination conscientiously and tackle the paper in a methodical manner, you won't need it!

indication of footnote

short prose quotation incorporated in the text of the essay, within quotation marks

setting up of rules and limits as *the* essential feature of play-activity. The educational psychologist Vygotsky, for example, argues that the pleasure of a game lies in choosing to submit to the rules. He says, 'The essential attribute of play is a rule that has become a desire'.[1] So, rules, limits, and finding pleasure in maintaining the game's order are crucial characteristics, especially of the very disciplined games mostly played in Highbury. Looked at in this light, the games in *Emma* begin to take on a possible new significance. To understand this, we need to look more carefully at Highbury society.

Highbury also functions by observing a strict set of rules and by maintaining a very particular order. There are a number of commonly held, unwritten 'laws' governing everyone and position. It is by observing these rules that the running of Highbury society is maintained. Marriage alliances are formed on the basis of these rules. Friendships formed within their limits. If these limits are overstepped even slightly, the strict social order of Highbury is threatened. Mr Knightley is worried by Emma's patronage of Harriet, for example, because he fears it will unsettle her and disturb the existing order. He says:

book title in italics. In a handwritten or typed manuscript this would appear as underlining : Emma.

> Hartfield will only put her out of conceit with all the other places she belongs to. She will grow just refined enough to be uncomfortable with those among whom birth and circumstances have placed her home.

(chapter 5)

long prose quotations idented and introduced a colon. Quotation marks are not needed.

The ball at the Crown Inn provides a good opportunity for a demonstration of the hierarchy that governs this order:

> Mr Weston and Mrs Elton led the way, Mr Frank Churchill Miss Woodhouse followed. Emma must submit to stand to Mrs Elton, though she had always considered peculiarly for her.

Chapter or page references should normally be given in assignment essays and in examination essays where a text is supplied.

These unwritten rules are never more obvious th Mrs Elton crudely insists on their observance. On the ill-

---

[1] L S Vygotsky, *Mind in Society* (Harvard, Massachusetts, 1978), p.99.

footnote, supplying bibliographical information as specified on pages 140–141

36

We have divided the following information into two sections. Part A describes those rules which it is essential to master no matter what kind of essay you are writing (including examination answers). Part B sets out some of the more detailed conventions which govern the documentation of essays.

PART A: LAYOUT

Titles of texts

Titles of published books, plays (of any length), long poems, pamphlets and periodicals (including newspapers and magazines), works of classical literature, and films should be underlined: e.g. David Copperfield (novel), Twelfth Night (play), Paradise Lost (long poem), Critical Quarterly (periodical), Horace's Ars Poetica (Classical work), Apocalypse Now (film).

Notice how important it is to distinguish between titles and other names. Hamlet is the play; Hamlet the prince. Wuthering Heights is the novel; Wuthering Heights the house. Underlining is the equivalent in handwritten or typed manuscripts of printed italics. So what normally appears in this volume as *Othello* would be written as Othello in your essay.

Titles of articles, essays, short stories, short poems, songs, chapters of books, speeches, and newspaper articles are enclosed in quotation marks; e.g. 'The Flea' (short poem), 'The Prussian Officer' (short story), 'Middleton's Chess Strategies' (article), 'Thatcher Defects!' (newspaper headline).

Exceptions: Underlining titles or placing them within quotation marks does not apply to sacred writings (e.g. Bible, Koran, Old Testament, Gospels) or parts of a book (e.g. Preface, Introduction, Appendix).

It is generally incorrect to place quotation marks around a title of a published book which you have underlined. The exception is 'titles within titles': e.g. 'Vanity Fair': A Critical Study (title of a book about *Vanity Fair*).

Quotations

Short verse quotations of a single line or part of a line should be incorporated within quotation marks as part of the running text of your essay. Quotations of two or three lines of verse are treated in the same way, with line endings indicated by a slash(/). For example:

1   In Julius Caesar, Antony says of Brutus, 'This was the noblest Roman of them all'.
2   The opening of Antony's famous funeral oration, 'Friends, Romans, Countrymen, lend me your ears;/ I come to bury Caesar not to praise him', is a carefully controlled piece of rhetoric.

Longer verse quotations of more than three lines should be indented from the main body of the text and introduced in most cases with a colon. Do not enclose indented quotations within quotation marks. For example:

It is worth pausing to consider the reasons Brutus gives to justify his decision to assassinate Caesar:

> It must be by his death; and for my part,
> I know no personal cause to spurn at him,
> But for the general. He would be crowned.
> How might that change his nature, there's the question.

At first glance his rationale may appear logical . . .

Prose quotations of less than three lines should be incorporated in the text of the essay, within quotation marks. Longer prose quotations should be indented and the quotation marks omitted. For example:

1   Before his downfall, Caesar rules with an iron hand. His political opponents, the Tribunes Marullus and Flavius, are 'put to silence' for the trivial offence of 'pulling scarfs off Caesar's image'.
2   It is interesting to note the rhetorical structure of Brutus's Forum speech:

> Romans, countrymen, and lovers, hear me for my cause, and be silent that you may hear. Believe me for my honour, and have respect to mine honour that you may believe. Censure me in your wisdom, and awake your senses, that you may the better judge.

Tenses: When you are relating the events that occur within a work of fiction, or describing the author's technique, it is the convention to use the present tense. Even though Orwell published *Animal Farm* in 1945, the book *describes* the animals' seizure of Manor Farm. Similarly, Macbeth always *murders* Duncan, despite the passage of time.

PART B: DOCUMENTATION

When quoting from verse of more than twenty lines, provide line references: e.g. In 'Upon Appleton House' Marvell's mower moves 'With whistling scythe and elbow strong' (l.393).

Quotations from plays should be identified by act, scene and line references: e.g. Prospero, in Shakespeare's The Tempest, refers to Caliban as 'A devil, a born devil' (IV.1.188). (i.e. Act 4. Scene 1. Line 188).

Quotations from prose works should provide a chapter reference and, where appropriate, a page reference.

Bibliographies should list full details of all sources consulted. The way is which they are presented varies, but one standard format is as follows:

1 Books and articles are listed in alphabetical order by the author's last name. Initials are placed after the surname.
2 If you are referring to a chapter or article within a larger work, you list it by reference to the author of the article or chapter, not the editor (although the editor is also named in the reference).
3 Give (in parentheses) the place and date of publication, e.g. (London, 1962). These details can be found within the book itself. Here are some examples:

> Brockbank, J. P., 'Shakespeare's Histories, English and Roman', in Ricks, C. (ed.) English Drama to 1710 (Sphere History of Literature in the English Language) (London, 1971).
> Gurr, A., 'Richard III and the Democratic Process', Essays in Criticism 24 (1974), pp. 39–47.
> Spivack, B., Shakespeare and the Allegory of Evil (New York, 1958).

Footnotes: In general, try to avoid using footnotes and build your references into the body of the essay wherever possible. When you do use them give the full bibliographic reference to a work in the first instance and then use a short title: e.g. See K. Smidt, <u>Unconformities in Shakespeare's History Plays</u> (London, 1982), pp. 43–47 becomes Smidt (pp. 43–47) thereafter. Do not use terms such as 'ibid.' or 'op. cit.' unless you are absolutely sure of their meaning.

There is a principle behind all this seeming pedantry. The reader ought to be able to find and check your references and quotations as quickly and easily as possible. Give additional information, such as canto or volume number whenever you think it will assist your reader.

SUGGESTIONS FOR FURTHER READING

Other works by Austen
Austen's five other completed novels — *Sense and Sensibility* (1811), *Pride and Prejudice* (1813), *Mansfield Park* (1814), *Northanger Abbey* (1818) and *Persuasion* (1818) — are all available in Penguin editions.

Also of interest is:

Chapman, R W (ed.), *Jane Austen: Selected Letters* (Oxford, 1955)

Biography
Cecil, D, *A Portrait of Jane Austen* (Harmondsworth, 1978)
Honan, P, *Jane Austen: Her Life* (London, 1987)

General studies of Austen's works, containing helpful chapters on *Emma*
Craik, W A, *Jane Austen: The Six Novels* (London, 1965)
Hardy, J, *Jane Austen's* Heroines (London, 1984)
Tanner, T, *Jane Austen* (London, 1986)
Williams, M., *Jane Austen: Six Novels and their Methods* (London, 1986)

Single-text studies of *Emma*
Bradbrook, F, *Emma* (Arnold Studies in English Literature; London, 1961)
Lodge, D (ed.), *Jane Austen: Emma* (Macmillan Casebook; London, 1968)

Longman Group UK Limited
*Longman House, Burnt Mill, Harlow, Essex, CM20 2JE, England
and Associated Companies throughout the World.*

First published 1988
ISBN 0 582 00653 8

*Set in 10/12 pt Century Schoolbook, Linotron 202
Printed in Great Britain by Bell and Bain Ltd., Glasgow*

Acknowledgement
The editors would like to thank Zachary Leader for his assistance with the style sheet.

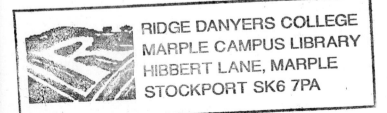